Love Betray'd

1703

A FACSIMILE PUBLISHED BY CORNMARKET PRESS
FROM THE COPY IN THE BIRMINGHAM SHAKESPEARE LIBRARY
LONDON
1969

PUBLISHED BY CORNMARKET PRESS LIMITED
42/43 CONDUIT STREET LONDON W1R ONL
PRINTED IN ENGLAND BY FLETCHER AND SON LIMITED NORWICH

SBN 7191 0190 5

Love Betray'd ;

OR, THE

Agreable Disapointment.

A

COMEDY.

As it was Acted at the

Theatre in *Lincolns-Inn-Fields.*

By the Author of *The Ladies Visiting-Day.*

Jam te sequetur.

LONDON:

Printed for D. Brown at the *Black-Swan* without *Temple-Bar,*
F. Coggan in the *Inner-Temple-Lane, Fleet-Street, W. Davis* at the
Black-Bull, and *G. Strahan* at the *Golden-Ball* against the *Ex-
change* in *Cornhill.* 1703.

THE
PREFACE.

PArt of the Tale of this Play, I took from *Shakespear*, and about Fifty of the Lines ; Those that are his, I have mark'd with Inverted Comma's, to distinguish 'em from what are mine. I endeavour'd where I had occasion to introduce any of 'em, to make 'em look as little like Strangers as possible, but am affraid (tho' a Military Critick did me the honour to say I had plunder'd all from *Shakespear*) that they wou'd easily be known without my Note of distinction.

The

The PREFACE.

The Conduct of the Drama I broke by defign, to make room for a Mask that is mention'd in the laft Act, but the Houfe neglecting to have it Set to Mufick, the Play came on like a change of Government, the weight of the Calamity fell among the Poor; that is, the chief Perfons only were taken care of without any regard to thofe of Inferiour confideration.

I endeavour'd to make the Converfation as general as it was poffible; but fince Infamy and Pride, Affectation and Singularity are the proper objects of this fort of Writing, it is very difficult to efcape the being thought Particular: The whole Herd are Alarm'd.

Sibi quifque timet quanquam eft intactus & odit.

A Perfon of this fort, I am told, has complain'd (to fome who were not fo proper to fatisfie him in it) that he is Difho-

Diſhonour'd by an Expreſſion in the Third
Act ; but his great tenderneſs in men-
tioning it to me, brings into my Thoughts
a Gentleman of ſo Nice Generoſity, that
he wou'd not ask a favour of a
certain great Man, becauſe he was ſure
he cou'd not deny it him.

As to the Place of the Scene, I confeſs I might have made a better choice
for the preſent condition of a Country,
is what firſt preſents it ſelf to us when
it is nam'd, and a Duke of *Venice* wou'd
be apt too appear too full of Years, and
Grey Hairs for a Lover, but ſeveral re-
volutions have afflicted that State, and
their Princes have ſometimes been Abſo-
lute.

For an Author not to Talk of his
Succeſſes, is reckon'd a very difficult mo-
deſty, and one may as well ſtop a He-
ro's Mouth after a Campaign, or a Tra-
vellor's after he's made the Tour of *Italy*! But 'tis a Secret as great, not to judge
of one's own Work, as not to Quarrel

at

at another's doing it ; for *there are cer-*
tainly no good Criticks, who are not
of our Opinion ; yet in general, I'll venture to fay of this fort of Writing, that
the Elaborate may Amufe us, and a Mon-
fter Surprize ! But 'tis Nature only that
will pleafe every body : The Picture has
an Affinity with the Life, and is ally'd
to our Senfes : It anfwers to fomething
we carry about us, and like an Inftrument
that's tun'd to another, touches us with
every found.

This confideration, I doubt not gave birth
to all thofe Wonders our Predeceffors Af-
crib'd to the power of Mufick : they were
not fatisfy'd with giving it a Dominion o-
ver reafonable Creatures, but extended its
Conqueft to Brutes and Trees. Nothing
was fecure againft its force, but that In-
fipid part of Mankind, whofe merit you
cant feperate from their Clothes, who
abominate Thinking and Foul Linnen, and
only fill up a Room in the World, who
tread the great Footfteps of *Penelope's*
Lovers.

Nos

The PREFACE.

Nos numerus sumus & fruges consumere nati.

They have been told that Nature gives us but few Pleasures, and that Reason robs us of some of those.

---

a   PROLOGUE

PROLOGUE,

Spoke by Mr. *Dogget*,

In a Lawyers Gown.

IF no difguife fhou'd pafs upon the Age,
  This wou'd be then the Habit of the Stage :
We Live on Plays, as Lawyers on a Caufe,
And both our bufinefs is to hide their Flaws :
We neither care if Cliant finks or fwims,
Nor ftruggle for the Caufe, but what it brings :
We have our Judges too-----fuch as they are ;
Some Frown ! fome Swell ! fome Nod too ! and fome Hear !
Tho' they can t See-----   ⌈The Upper Gallery.
No Cliant can their ftubborn Virtue move,
Yet fome Intelligence with us they Love.
To us the Learned in the Law they'll yield,
And lengthen out the Harveft of the Field :
Our Fiddles, Songs and Dances, are Sham Pleas,
To baffle Juftice, and to bring in Fees :
Our dirty Mobb, and all the Rabble Rout,
Are----- Attorneys ! Bayliffs ! Clerks ! that clog the Court,
And liftening Councel !-----

                                        When

When you our *Judges* come, the *Court* is *Set*,
And chance determins every *Poet's Fate* :
We both love *Forms*, that have been fettled once well,
And ftill with *Prologue Speaks*----the opening *Councel.*
My Lord! this *Caufe* is evident ! fpeaks for it felf *my Lord!*
And fome---I beg your *Lordfhip's Ear* for half a word.
So we *Stage Councels*, with the fame defign,
Open our *Caufe*, fome *Strut* too, and fome *Whine* :.
As we and *Lawyers* thus exactly match,
Let not our *Court* be fcandal'd for difpatch ;
But with the fame amufing *Wifdom* paufe,
And *Spin* the *Tryal*, tho' you *Damn* the *Caufe.*

a 2   E P I-

EPILOGUE,

Spoke by Mrs. *Barry*.

OUR Marriages we see are made above,
   And not directed for the thing we Love;
But tho' I'm pleas'd, must some Reflections make,
That much allay this lucky strange mistake:
My Husband, had he Wit, might fear, again
Another Man may do as much by him!
Excuses too will never be believ'd!
For here ----few Women are, but once deceiv'd:
Yet no suspicion in his Climate thrives,
The French----are never Jealous of their Wives:
Marriage in this, for Women does decree;
The Knot is Wove with so much subtlety,
That 'tis the Husband's Interest not to see:
He can't our Shame, without his own disclose,
So much 'tis at his Peril, if he knows!
Thus Nature wisely for our Peace provides,
And from the Men, her tender Secrets hides:
To Live in Ignorance she makes their store;
But Woman's happiness in knowing more:

Yet

Yet a strange Star, when she was Born must shine,
Whose Joy's secur'd by crossing her design!
A different Fate the Lover was allow'd,
Who sought a Substance, and imbrac'd a Cloud:
For me the Substance for the Cloud is lay'd;
Was ever Love so civilly betray'd?
No disapointment ever was so kind;
Or Woman so much cheated to her mind!

DRA

Books Printed for *D. Brown*, at the *Black-Swan* without *Temple-Bar*.

BEam's Duel, or a Souldier for the Ladies.

The Monument, a Poem on the moft Lamented Death of the ever Glorious King William, by Mr. *Dennis*.

Art of Prudence, or a Companion for a man of Senfe, Tranflated from the Spanifh, of the Famous Grecian, with the Notes of Amelont de la Houfa, by Mr. *Savage*.

Arts of Improvement, in a Collection of Experiments, from the beft Authors Manufcript, &c. by E. S.

Books Printed for *Fran. Coggan*, in the *Inner-Temple-Lane*.

PRefent State of Mufcovy, to the Year 1699.

Hiftory of the laft Parliament, began at *Weftminfter* the 10th of *February* 1700. by Dr. *Drake*, the 2d Edit.

Hiftory of Germany, from the Foundation of the Empire, to this prefent time, containing the Lives of all the Emperours, and an Account of the prefent State thereof, with the Heads of all the Emperours to this time. In 2 Vol. by Mr. *Savage*.

Princefs of Cleve, a fam'd Romance.

Zade, a Romance, Tranflated out of Spanifh.

Conveyancer's Affiftant and Director.

Law of Corporation.

PLAYS.

Innocent Miftrefs.

Fatal Friendfhip.

Triumphant Widow, or the Medley of Humours, by the D. of *Newcaftle*

Guzman, a Comedy, by the Lord *Orrery*.

Fools Preferment, or the 3 Dukes of Dunftable.

Oroonoko.

Perjur'd Husband.

Bath, or the Weftern Lafs.

Pyrhus, King of Epirus.

Boadicia, Queen of Britain.   } All by Mr. *Hopkins*.

Female Warriour.

Rinaldo and Armida.

Plot and No Plot.

Dramatis Personæ.

MEN.

Moreno,	Mr. Verbrugen.
Drances,	Mr. Powell.
Sebaſtian,	Mr. Booth.
Taquilet,	Mr. Dogget.
Rodoregue,	Mr. Fieldhouſe.
Pedro,	Mr. Pack.

WOMEN.

Villaretta,	Mrs. Bracegirdle.
Cæſario,	Mrs. Prince.
Dromia,	Mrs. Leigh.
Lawra,	Mrs. Lawſon.

Officers and Attendants.

Love

ACT I.

SCENE, a House in *Venice*.

Enter Villaretta, *and* Emilia, *follow'd by a Page at a distance.*

Em. HA! ha! ha! ha! ha! I shall die! ha! ha! oh! hold me——

Vill. Here! here! take the Sots Cordial; a little of the same—— read on and live——

(gives her a Letter)

Em. Ha! ha! ha! This Letter has something in it! I wish a Lover of mine wou'd write so—— I shou'd like it far beyond your charming Shapes, pretty Mouths, or all the fine Eyes in the World—— such Compliments are meer Whip-cream to this.

Vill. You are smitten *Emilia!*

Em. Why he writes the finest in the World! and there's not a Woman in *Venice*, except your Ladyship, but wou'd be smitten too—— let's see if it be possible to resist such Eloquence.

(reads)

B

Madam,

Madam,

I love you very much ; as a proof of my Sincerity, I am worth Two hundred thousand Cechines, and will settle all to reconcile you to the Name of

ANTONIO.

Vill. A saucy Fellow!

Em. Nay then I don't know what you call Civil——I never saw such a well-bred Letter in my Life. I love a Banker's inditing! When shou'd one hear a Courtier say so? I wonder you are not mov'd at it, and a Widow too!

Vill. 'Tis for that reason! The greatest Happiness of our Lives, is to have got free from the Mens Dominion very early; they are all Tyrants——

Em. If the Piece indeed be as bad as your Pattern.

Vill. It must be so; all Husbands are the same; Love makes 'em our Prisoners, and Jealousy our Goalers; so between these two, a poor Woman has no quiet——

Em. Till they are dead.

Vill. Ha! ha! right *Emilia*; the Grave gives more People rest, than those it holds—— take care you don't want that comfort.

Em. I fear it not—— because you have burnt your Mouth, shan't keep me from tasting—— I'll venture upon a Man, in spite of all the Terror about him-- in a Province of *Italy* too.

Vill. The worst Place in the World to marry in; if one wou'd be a Mistress, I shou'd chuse *Italy*; If a Wife, *England*, but a Maid shou'd live in *France*, for
there

there she may have all the Enjoyments of the other two, and keep her Character.

Em. Upon such terms indeed one might live a Maid all ones Life.

Vill. Ha ! ha ! without repining at leading Apes hereafter.

Em. The Curse wou'd be a little moderated.

Vill. With these Principles, *Emilia*, you may pass your time well enough, be your Tyrant ever so much an *Italian* ; for Love will always be too cunning for Jealousy.

Em. Nay if he suspected my Virtue, the first thing I'd do, shou'd be to lose it—— If he set a Spy of his own Sex upon me, as many Husbands do, I'd find a way to bribe my Keeper, as all Wives do—— And if he lock'd me up---

Vill. You cou'd have no way left---

Em. But Imagination--- and that shou'd revenge me every Minute.

Vill. Spoke like the Spirit of our Sex ! I find the Men will get nothing by opposing us, we are all *English* by Nature, and to flatter us, is the best way to enslave us--- But to avoid the hazzard, I'll treat all Men as I do this Fellow--- Page ! bear this back to *Antonio*, and tell him, if he has the assurance to write again, I'll have his Ears taken off, and nail'd up in the *Ryalto*.

(Exit Page with a Letter)

Em. Well now cou'd not I for my Heart have sent such an Answer to a Compliment of 200 thousand--- Why the Duke himself don't say finer things to you.

Vill. I seldom mind what he says, and the reason I don't quite put him off, is, because it pleases me to govern him that governs *Venice*.

B 2

Em.

Em. I fhou'd not venture fo far--- Beauty's an Empire that won't laft always.

Vill. As long as I live *Emilia*--- When knew you a rich Womans-Face have any Wrinkles, or a rich Man's Head any Folly?

Em. Then the Banker's muft be an ingenious one.

Vill. Name him no more--- fuch a greafy Fellow next my Stomach, is enough to give me the Spleen all Day.

Em. What with fo much Gold about him? I'm told it's the beft Cure of it in the World, and brightens the Complexion--- No body has the Spleen but old Women, and younger Brothers--- Say what you will, *Villaretta*, a Banker has his Charms.

Vill. But fhe that weds for thofe Charms, may find her felf ne'er the Handfomer.

Em. I'm ftrangely deceived then-- for tho' they'll give little, yet they'll truft one with all; and I fhou'd fcarce be the firft Steward that did not provide for my felf.

Vill. Nay, you're a States-man's Daughter, and they never were concern'd in the Government, that can tell Money and be poor, Cofen.

Em. But Husbands, I fear, reckon better than the Publick. And if after ten Years Managery, I fhou'd be fo unfortunate to be found out.

Vill. The Calamity wou'd come too late. The Steward wou'd be too great for the Lord.

Em. Yet there wou'd be fome little Flaws in our Character.

Vill. Not if there were none in your Eftate.

Em. I like your Philofophy extreamly--- why this is Virtue all Woman-kind may follow--- But to be grave, thefe Men, after all, have made a poor Woman's Conduct fo difficult, that moft of our Pleafures clafh with

our

our Reputation.--- 'tis not so with them; they may do any thing, and yet be Men of Honour.

Vill. Those that make Laws will always favour themselves. They have made their own Honour confist in Bravery, which is for their advantage; but ours to confist in Chastity, which is not for ours.

Em. If we had order'd things, it had been the Mens part to be Modest, Faithful, Reserved, and hating every thing they desired, and ours to ha' done what we please.

Vill. The World had been much better govern'd that's certain--- Why shou'd a pack of Bald-pated, shriveled old Fellows, give Laws to us that are young and handsome?

Em. So Arbitarily too--- They have left us nothing-- but the power of deceiving 'em.

Vill. And that no body can take from a Woman.

Em. 'Tis pretty well employ'd too--- for we look upon their Ordinances, as a Lawyer does upon a new Statute, not to mind the intent of it, but to find a hole to creep out at.

Vill. Ha! ha! and I have been told that 'tis impossible to make 'em so binding, but one may find some, *Emilia.*

Em. Ha! ha! yet how can we get over so palpable a Law, as *Wives be true to your Husbands.*

Vill. O! by making them get over as palpable a Condition; *Husbands love your Wives*; which now you know is not the Fashion.

Enter a Foot-man.

Foot. Madam, The Duke of *Venice* desires to wait upon your Ladyship.

Vill.

Vill. Let him ſtay--- I an't at leiſure yet---

(*Exit Foot.*)

This mighty Man, *Emilia*, comes ſo often, I ſhall be tired with laughing at him--- I'll e'en give him his Anſwer, as my Woman calls it.

Em. People might diſpence with your leavings ; the Banker, and the Duke; all Women han't ſuch Lovers to throw away---

Vill. All Lovers are alike to me, *Emilia*, they're Men ; and when a Hypocrite is known, 'tis ridiculous to ſee him practice his ſoft Airs, forc'd Languiſhments, and low Bows:

Em. Soft ! here's the Duke.

Vill. Then for an Inſtance.

Enter Moreno, *bowing very low.*

Mor. Madam, I come to prove *Moreno*'s Fate:
This Day has been propitious to our Race ;
My Father on it triumph'd o'er the *Turks*,
And gain'd the loſt *Morea* to the State.
Moreno's Fortune may be great as his,
If Heaven and *Villaretta* will be kind.

Vill. Still upon this Subject, my Lord--- ? you know my Mind ; that I aſſure you is not Woman, for it ſhall never alter--- ſo no more, my Lord.

Mor. Yet hear me, Madam, I do not offer you a Wretch, a Vagabond, an Out-law.

Vill. No ! a Duke of *Venice*.

(*ſmiling*)

Mor. Madam, I plead no merit from my Fortune ; all Honour vaniſhes before the Fair ; and all are mean to *Villaretta*'s Eyes.

Em.

Em. (*Aside*) The poor Man is certainly in earnest !

Mor. Nay, I wou'd for ever quit all Glory, Friends, the World, if to lose those Trifles, I shou'd gain your Favour.

Vill. No promising, my true Lord ; but cease this whining Entertainment, and when we meet, let us have no Speeches with Sighs at the end of 'em.

Em. (*Aside to her*) Well ! if he has half so much Modesty as Passion, I'll answer for your quiet hereafter--

Vill. No bleeding Heart, soft Sonnet, purling Streams, nor such like melancholy Things.

Mor. (*Aside*) That I cou'd tear the Tyrant from my Breast. A true Merciless, Insolent--- Charming Woman--- !

Em. (*to* Vill.) Cousen *Drances* drunk, as I live !

Enter Drances.

Dra. My Lord, I'm yours.

Mor. Segnior *Drances*---

Vill. (*Aside*) One Fool is enough at once---

(*fretting*)

Dra. What my Cousen in her moods ? My Lord, don't mind her--- If you had been as deep in the Cellar as I have, you wou'd not care a Fig for her--- The Jade is a Virtue, my Lord, and I never knew a Woman have the least good Nature, that had any Honesty, by *Jupiter*.

Em. I believe, Sir, your Acquaintance are very good Natured.

Dra. Well said Coz. ! My Lord, I'm no Sinner, if I had not once a strong Inclination to strain a Commandment with that fresh colour'd Cousen of mine--- She's a pretty Wench, and Flesh and Blood you know--- But my dear Lord be merry.

Mor.

Mor. That from *Villaretta*, wou'd make me so for ever.

Vill. Then I desire it my Lord, and leave you to't for ever.

(*Exeunt* Em. *and* Vill.)

Mor. She's gone, and all that's happy with her.

Dra. Let her go, my Lord--- Hang these Women, they're never good Company when there's more than one Man in the Room with 'em.

Mor. You're a happy Man, *Drantes*--- when shall I have your Quiet ?

Dra. When you drink like me--- Sit but a Hand out, my Lord--- All the Joys in Nature lie in the second Bottle; your Groves, and Streams, and Nightingales--- and twenty things besides Women with black Eyes.

Mor. If *Villaretta* appear'd there, I'd drink for ever.

Dra. Live with me, my Lord, and try--- Ha ! ha ! my Kinswoman and I, you must know, divide the House ; all under-ground is mine ; the whole Region of Mirth and Claret. I can't look upward without a Tres-pass--- Ha ! ha ! I happened to whisper her House-maid, that I had fallen in love with one Morning at Prayers, and she sent her to the Devil immediately, for I never saw her after.

Mor. Where cou'd you fly for that Day.

Dra. To the Curate's Comfort, my Lord ; a Bottle and a Pipe ; for grief is never eas'd so well, as when its drown'd ; try it my Lord, drink, and remember *Villaretta* no more.

Mor. (*Sighs*)

Dra. Don't sigh, my Lord, it has a dead Sound, there's some Musick now in a Hick-up.

Mor.

Mor. What can I do, when *Villaretta* is so cruel?

Dra. Do, my Lord! why you go the wrong way to do any thing with a Widow---

Mor. If my Love and Services won't recommend me--

Dra. Potguns! they may do well enough with a Maid-- A Country unus'd to War, and eafily furpriz'd; but a Widow's a fortify'd Town, that has had Enemies before it, and will never be taken, my Lord, without you bring down the great Guns upon it.

Mor. But in Love, *Drances*, we muſt all fight like *French*-men; if we can't bribe the Governour, we ſhall never come at the Garriſon.

Dra. Well, my Lord, to ſerve you, and to divert a Miſtreſs of mine--- for *Cupid* has been playing about the Edges of my Glaſs, and juſt put in the tip of his Arrow--- 'tis but a ſlight Wound; *Dromia's* Darts han't kill'd out-right---

Mor. Not theſe 50 Years: Why you had better marry your Grand-mother: She'll neither adminiſter to your Happineſs nor Mirth.

Dra. But ſhe makes the beſt Water-gruel in the World--- Others marry to have more Care, but I to be taken care off--- The diverſion is, I have told the Butler, (who is a very ſilly Fellow, my Lord,) that my Couſin is in Love with him.

Mor. And how did it move him?

Dra. As Sack and Sugar does a Midwife--- He lick'd his Lips immediately, and ſent for a Taylor to make him a Gentleman.

Mor. To make him a Gentleman?

Dra. Ay, my Lord, they make more in a Year than the Heralds-Office, or a *Welch* Genealogiſt; eſpecially your pretty Gentlemen are all made ſo---

Mor. But how will this ſerve me?

C   *Dra.*

Dra. It will beat down her Pride, the grand Bulwork, that defends more Women than Virtue--- But follow me into the Cellar, and I'll tell you more--- I never speak well without a Flask under my Arm; for as the Chaplain says; *The Dry are always Dull.*

Mor. (*Aside*) No body's so fit to keep a Sot Company, as he that's deny'd *Villaretta's.*

(*Exeunt*)

Enter Cæfario *and* Laura.

Scene changes to the Duke's House.

Cæf. Prithee Wench lay by thy Fears.
Laur. Alas! Madam, it grieves me to think that my Lady must be a Servant, that may be so waited on! To be a Page, and wear Breeches too!

(*weeps*)

Cæf. You talk like a Woman, *Laura,* I must make you wear Breeches too, to be less fearful.
Laur. Oh! dear Madam, ha! ha! your Ladyship makes me laugh.
Cæf. This Servitude is Freedom, for it brings me to the Man I love--- The little Spot that holds him, *Laura,* is all the Liberty I ask; the World without it is a Prison.
Laur. Nay, Love is a parlous Thing, I know Madam--- I was troubled with it once, and remember well I cou'd not sleep a Nights! but it went off in a Week, for I found he had not Money enough.
Cæf. Ha! ha! poor *Laura!* then you'd ha' broke your Heart for him, if he had had Money enough?

Laur.

Laur. 'Twou'd ha' been bad with me I believe; but when a Sweetheart is poor, Madam, 'tis as hard to Love, as to be Charitable.

Cæf. Ha! ha! ha! This Wench will kill me with her extreme Stupidity! ha! ha!

Laur. Lord, Madam! you look so like your Brother when you laugh, and in these Cloaths too, that, I vow, I can't tell but you are my Master *Sebastian*, all this while.

Cæf. 'Twou'd puzzel one of better Sense than thee, *Laur i*, to distinguish it--- for besides our likeness, I have dreft my self as he use to do; but to put you out of doubt, behold the only apparent difference between us, this Mole!

(bares her Arm)

Laur. O my dear Lady *Viola!* 'tis you, I know it now--- The Duke, Madam, took me with him, to wait upon his Sifter, and I have liv'd here ever since--- I little thought to see your Ladyship my Fellow-servant---!

(weeps)

Cæf. I'm greater now, than when I was thy Mistrefs.

Laur. I hope my Lord is kind to you, for he charges us all to be fo--- But, dear Madam, how could you venture to do this? I'm in a Maze yet!

Cæf. I'll tell thee all, because thou should'ft not trouble me with more Queftions, and because I love to fpeak of him.

Laur. (*Afide*) That's the trueft Reafon, I know by my felf.

Cæf. I faw him firft in *France*, and lov'd him; these two Years I have lov'd him; unable longer to endure the torture of my Wifhes, I left my Brother, and

C 2 my

my Houſe, and 6 Days ſince, without a Servant, landed here in *Venice*——

Lau. Your Ladyſhip makes me weep again.

Cæſ. I nam'd my ſelf *Caſario*, and form'd a Letter, as from one his Highneſs knew in *Paris*, to recommend me for his Page.·- Upon it, *Laura*, he receiv'd me; lik'd my Perſon; calls me pretty Youth; makes me ſing to him, and ſometimes kiſſes me.

Lau. Then you are happy, Madam.

Cæſ. If it were meant me as a Woman; but he kills me while he makes me happy, for in the midſt of all, he ſighs, and talks to me of a Lady that he loves.

Lau. Nay, then all's marr'd again.

Cæſ. But ſhe is cruel to him, and hates him.

Lau. That's good again, Madam. Have you ſeen this Lady?

Cæſ. No, but he has told me who ſhe is, and deſigns to ſend me with a Meſſage to her.

Lau. Its like to be done well, if you carry it--- But how can you do any thing for your ſelf, Madam? 'Twill be impoſſible for him to ſee a Woman, as they ſay, thro' a Pair of Breeches.

Cæſ. No more than thro' a Nun's Habit--- When I find a proper time for my purpoſe, a little thing will ſhew him what I am.

Lau. I ſhall die with Joy if it ſo happens! Your Ladyſhip will be happy indeed; for his Highneſs is a ſort of King here.

Cæſ. Is that to be happy indeed, *Laura?*

Lau. O! dear Madam, without queſtion: I admire a King ſo much, that I cou'd marry one, that had only a Twelfth-Cake for his Dominions.

Cæſ. Ha! ha! a ſmall Country! but in *Italy* you may find fifty ſuch Princes--- Ha! ha! prithee, *Laura*, how would'ſt thou govern thy little Nation?

Lau.

Lau. As Princes (in thofe Parts) generally do, Madam ; devour as much as I cou'd of it.

Cæf. You are the firft Monarch that ever was fo free.

Lau. Pardon me, Madam, I forgot I was talking to your Ladyfhip.

Cæf. Nay, then 'tis plain you'd make a good Governour, for thou feeft nothing but what thou look'ft upon, poor *Laura !* --- Hold, I'm call'd, now we muft be private Perfons again.

(*within,* Cæfario, Cæfario.)

Enter *Footman.*

Foot. O ! here he is--- Sir, the Duke is come home very much out of Humour, and wants you immediately.

Cæf. Doeft know the Caufe of his Diforder?

Foot. No Sir ; he came from the Lady *Villaretta's,* and feems to be very fick.

(*Exit Foot.*)

Cæf. Hum ! --- I come.

He muft be ficker yet, e'er I am well,
And feel the laft Convulfions of Defpair---
But Love muft work this wonder in his Breaft,
And Banifh quite that happy Woman thence :
Shew me the foft Avenues to his Heart ;
His Soul unruffl'd, every Thought at eafe :
A lucky Hour may all my Toils repair,
When I may talk of Love, and he may hear !

Exeunt.

End of the firft A C T.

A C T

ACT II.

SCENE *opens, and discovers* Moreno *on a Couch, and* Cæsario *kneeling by----*

Cæsario sings.

I.

IF *I hear* Orinda *Swear,*
    She cures my jealous Smart;
The Treachery becomes the Fair,
    And doubly fires my Heart.

II.

Beauty's Strength and Treasure,
    In Falshood still remain;
She gives the greatest Pleasure,
    That gives the greatest Pain.

(*Soft Musick, after which,* Moreno *rises.*)

Mor. " If Musick be the Food of Love, play on !
" Give me excess of it, that surfeiting
" The Appetite, may sicken, and so die.
But oh ! in vain, the pleasing Sounds once o'er
Are lost for ever---- ! no Memory recalls
The Pleasure past, but that which wounds us lives !
How true a Wretch is Man ?
The mute Creation Nature has supply'd,
With Arts and Arms for their Defence and Safety ;
The Deer has Horns, and Subtlety the Fox,

The

The Porcupine ftill bears upon his Back.
A Grove of Arrows to diftrefs his Foe;
But the unhappy Lord of all is made,
With Darts turn'd inward on himfelf,
His own Deftroyer.......
His Paffions and his Faculties are given,
To war with his own Quiet--- Oh Diftraction !
Let me embrace thee......
For only they are happy who are Mad !

(Throws himfelf on the Couch)

Cæf. (Afide) Alas ! I pity his Diftrefs,
Tho' I'm overjoy'd at the occafion-- My Lord try to fleep.

Mor. Poor *Cæfario !* thou art too young for Cares,
Or thou hadft known, they follow us in Sleep.
Phyficians poyfon in their Sleep,
Lawyers undoe in their Sleep,
Courtiers get new Grants in their Sleep---
Nothing in Nature's quite at reft,
But the flick Prelate---

Cæf. Right ! my Lord, and the other Sex have their
Fancies too--- Old Women Back-bite and Pray in their
Sleep ; Young-ones Sigh and Dance in their Sleep ;
and Maids of thirty fet up for Virtue, and Drefs in
their Sleep.

Mor. Pretty Boy ! Thy Manners are fo foft, thy
Senfe fo quick at every turn ; thou fhould'ft be older
than thou feem'ft to be--- Haft ever been in Love ?

Cæf. A little my Lord---

Mor. 'Tis that has form'd thy Mind,
For Love, the kind refiner of the Soul,
Softens harfh Nature's Work, and tempers Man :
Without it, all are Salvages---
What fort of Woman ?

Cæf. One very like your Lordfhip.

Mor. By fo much the lefs meriting-- Did fhe love you ?

Cæf. She kift me often, and told me fo, but did not love
me.   *Mor.*

Mor. Truft 'em no more, they're all---

Cæf. O! hold, my Lord, fome are Juft, and Love as well as we. " My Father had a Daughter lov'd a Man, " As it might be, perhaps, were I a Woman, " I fhou'd your Highnefs.

Mor. And what's her Story?

Cæf. " A Blank, my Lord--- She never told her Love, " But let Concealment, like a Worm i'th' Bud, " Feed on her Damask Cheek---

——————————————She languifh'd long, Courting the Shade, the Night ftill found her weeping, Nor cou'd the Sun e'er dry her Tears away, 'Till pining with diftrefsful Melancholy " She fate like Patience on a Monument, fmiling at Grief. Reduced to thefe extreams, at laft I--- *(She blufhes)*

Mor. How's that, *Cæfario?*

Cæf. I don't--- you forget, my Lord, to fend me to the Lady. *(fhewing a Letter)*

Mor. Right! my dear Boy, go bear it to her now, And plead thy felf the Caufe of Love and Me; Thou haft a foft infinuating Way, May footh her Anger, and delude her Scorn. But if her People fhou'd deny thee entrance--

Cæf. I warrant ye, my Lord, I get admittance; I'll Storm the Houfe, and Beat the Servants; my Youth, and your Indulgence will protect me.

Mor. Nay; Women, Children, and Priefts, they fay, can affront no body, fo thou art fafe.

Cæf. O! very fafe, my Lord, doubly fafe.

Mor. Dear *Cæfario,* take this and profper, *(kiffes her)* Urge my Paffion to her, and my Faith.

Cæf. As zealoufly, as if your Favour depended on the Succefs; and if Fortune is but kind ————

Mor. Invoke thy own good Stars, for I have none.

Cæf. Moft faithfully, my Lord, and hope this Affair will be govern'd by 'em. *(Exeunt feverally)*

Scene

Scene changes to Villaretta*'s*

Enter Villaretta, Emilia, *and* Dromia, *(taking her leave)*

Dro. Nay, pray Ladies! Not a Step for me——
I'm gone in a moment. *(turns and returns)*

Vill. We will fee you to the Stairs, Madam.

Dro. I befeech your Ladyfhip-- Nay good Lady *Emilia.*

Em. Pray Madam——

Dro. You make me rude-- Your Servant-- Oh! dear--
pray--- My Service to Segnior *Drances.* *(Exit Dro.)*

Vill. Ha! ha! this old Woman is the very Pink of
Breeding, by her excefs of Civility, fhe fhou'd ha' been
bred a Manteau-maker.

Em. She thinks it the Character of Age to be Auftere,
and therefore hurries her poor Bones about, tho' they rat-
tle as much as if they were already made into Dice.

Vill. My Service to Segnior Drances! Ha! ha! I always
told you, that this old Fool had ftill a fnatch of 15 about her.

Em. And will carry't to her Grave, except our merry
Kinfman reels into her Arms.

Vill. His Liquor 'll defend him, for drunken Men, they
fay, come by no harm.

Em. It may be a good —— fhe'll cure his Intem-
perance, my Life for't.

Vill. She may be miftaken in her Remedy ---! I have
known People of her Age, marry with hopes of working
ftrange Cures upon their Husbands.

Em. And how did they fucceed?

Vill. As other Phyfitians, they grew their greateft
Difeafe.

Em. Which wou'd laft all their Lives too perhaps----
Well! methinks Marriage fhou'd end juft when People
began to hate one another.

Vill. At that rate you'd have few laft longer than a
monthly Rofe.

Em. If it fmells fweet for the time, its well enough-- I'd
fain have the Men make one Law that we like.

D   *Enter*

Enter a Footman.

Foot. Madam, a young Gentleman at the Gate defires to fpeak with you—— He is very importunate, tho' we told him you wou'd not be feen.

Vill. What fort of Perfon?

Foot. A very handfome Youth. [*Enter 2d Footman.*]

2d Foot. There's a Gentleman at the Gate, Madam, that fwears he muft fpeak with you, and will fpeak with you —— I told him, you were fick ; he fays he is a Doctor, and came to cure you ; I faid you were afleep, he knows that too, and comes to wake you : I don't know what to fay to him, he's prepar'd againft all Denials.

Vill. Hum ! Tell him he fhan't fpeak with me.

2d Foot. I have, Madam, but he fays he'll bring his Bed to the Door, and Live there till he does

Vill. A merry Fellow !

1ft Foot. He'll fpeak with your Ladyfhip in fpite of your Teeth.

Vill. I'll difappoint him—— Bid him come in.

1ft Foot. Come in, Madam ?

Vill. Yes, Impertinent.   (*Exeunt Footmen*)
Some Meffage from his Highnefs !

Em. Taken his Bed, and defires to fee you before he dies ! For after fuch a Repulfe, he can't in Gallantry live above two Hours.

Vill. Ha ! ha ! ha ! There is nothing fo ill-laid, as a Lover's-Plot—— no body's furpriz'd in it, but thofe that wou'd be taken--- Ha ! ha ! Well ! *Emilia,* the happyeft Woman in the World, is fhe that's a little Handfome ; no Fool ; and that never loves.   [*Enter* Cæfario]
Ha ! a handfome Youth.

Cæf. My Bufinefs is with the Lady of the Houfe

Vill. Then you may tell it me, Sir.

Cæf. (*Afide*) I'm loft ! She's beautiful indeed---! I fhan't be able to fpeak to her---

Em. (*to* Vill,) A pretty blufhing Boy !

Cæf.

Cæf. (*Afide*) But Woman affift me--- I'll belie my Heart, and look pleas'd.

Vill. A very filent Embaffy ! Sir, my Servants told me you had a Tongue.

Cæf. O! Madam, and a Heart, and Hands, and Legs, and all at your Ladyfhip's Service.

Vill. Then, Sir, pray employ the moft impertinent of 'em, and tell me your Bufinefs.

Cæf. Never apprehend my Tongue, Madam, 'tis as glib as a Woman's, and when once well in, will never lie ftill--- fo take a Husband's care not to fet it a going.

Vill. (*to* Em.) I don't know what's the matter, but I can't be angry with this faucy Boy--- Then, Sir, I muft not know the Bufinefs

Cæf. Yes, Lady, you muft know, but only you muft know it-- I muft have you by your felf, without a Witnefs.

Em. I go---

Vill. Hold--- Why, Sir, is it Treafon ?

Cæf. You prophane it with the comparifon. Treafon's a Proftitute, the Chat of every Table; but this, Madam, is fecret as Maiden-wifhes, I fcarce can truft it with my felf.

Vill. Emilia, I beg you to retire a little then, and let this impertinent Boy have his way.   (*Exit* Em.)

Cæf. Moft bountiful Lady ! were you as indulgent to Merit, as you are to Curiofity, this trouble had not been.

Vill. Well, Sir, the Bufinefs in as few Words as you can.

Cæf. Nay, Madam, I muft ufe more Words than I wou'd to tell it you.

Vill. Riddles--- !

Cæf. I come from a Lover to you.

Vill. Thou art as impertinent, as if thou wert one thy felf.

Cæf. But this Letter muft fpeak firft.

Vill. (*opens it*) Here, Sir, the laft Word is all I value in't, and not value in it, fo take it agen--- You, I fuppofe then, are his Page ?

Cæf. Yes, Madam, and fo have a Charter to be impudent.

Vill.

Vill. (*Aside*) 'Tis impoffible to be out of humour with this Youth--- What does the Boy look at ?

Cæf. To fee if all be Nature that I fee.

Vill. All in grain, I affure you Sir.

Cæf. " And will you lead thefe Graces to the Grave, " and leave the World no Copy ?

Vill. By no means, Sir, I'll have 'em inventori'd out, when I die, and added as a Label to my Will, that every one may know what I was poffeft of.

Cæf. Some know it too well already.

Vill. Prithee, who are they ?

Cæf. Why your Ladyfhip, and my Lord.

Vill. You put thofe together, that fhall never come together.

Cæf. Nay, Madam, I wou'd not put you together, Heaven knows ! And yet I muft tell you, that he loves you to that degree---

Vill. (*Aside*) I love to hear him talk, tho' one I hate is the Subject--- To what degree, Sir ?

Cæf. Why he talks of nothing but *Villaretta*, Dreams of nothing but *Villaretta*--- He Swears, and Smiles, Frets, and Dances like a *French*-man, in a Fit of the Spleen--- Then he thinks all the World Fools for being unconcern'd, but they, in return, think as oddly of him--- there's all the World to one, Madam !

Vill. Do you laugh at your Mafter ?

Cæf. No, Madam, I only laugh at a Mad-man, that raves of *Villaretta*-- My Mafter muft not be one that loves you--- When he fighs for you, I'm difcharg'd, but when he rails at you, I'm his humbleft Servant.

Vill. Why you and I are of a Mind ! I fhou'd bear him too, if he hated me, for I do him moft conftantly.

Cæf. I wou'd not truft you--- A Woman's Refolution is no more to be depended on, than a Man's Oath.

Vill. (*Aside*) I'm extremely pleas'd with this Youth--! Harky'e, Sir, what Country are you ? What Parentage ?

Cæf. " Above my Fortunes, yet my State is well ; " I am a Gentleman, my Name *Cæfario*------

But

But my Master, Lady, is the Theme ; you shou'd enquire how he rested... How he looks... And drop a little Pity on his Wounds... This, were I the Duke of *Venice*, I shou'd expect.

Vill. You might.... (*Aside*) What am I doing--! But tell your Master, I detest his Passion ; so let him trouble me no more, except, Sir, you'll call again, to tell me how he takes it... In the mean time, for your trouble, pray accept of this...   (*offers a Purse, &c.*)

Cæs. "(*putting away her Hand*) I am no fee'd Post, Madam, you misplace your Bounty—— "My Master, "not my self, wants recompence.   (*Exit.*)

Vill. Triumphant Honesty ! What is this Youth ? Above my Fortunes, yet my State is well ; I am a Gentleman—— For that, fair Youth, thou need'st no Herauld — That Tongue ! That Face ! That Spirit above Gain ! cou'd not be born of vulgar Parents——— ! Tho' he has left me, yet he is not gone, I feel him in my Breast dispensing Laws, And all within me pleas'd with his Commands. But hold... He does not know it—— Something I must do, or I may lose him... But *Villaretta*'s Youth and Fortune need not fear a disappointment... Yet to be sure.... here !

Enter Servant.

Run after that same saucy Youth, the Duke's Page.... He calls himself *Cæsario*... He threw this Ring at my Feet, as he went out, and left it, whether I would or not ; pray give it him again, and tell him, I shall be very angry if he plays these Tricks with me... He may, perhaps, have the Confidence to deny it ; but be sure you leave it ; and if he has any thing to say for himself, to excuse what he has done, you may bid him call to Morrow.

Serv. I will, Madam.   (*Exit Servant*)

Vill. I do I do'nt know what, and am asham'd, but Love must hide the blushes that he makes.   (*Exit*)

Scene

Scene changes to the Ryalto.

Enter Rodoregue, Sebaftian, *and* Pedro.

Rod. Dear *Sebaftian*, (tho' unknown to me before this
Voyage, yet fince our common Calamity has made us
one, let me call you fo) add not to the Miferies the Sea
has caus'd, by being fad.

Seb. Captain, your Friendfhip wou'd make me forget
any Lofs--- But a Sifters !

Rod. Since that may poffibly not be,
Diffide not in the Powers that guard her Life.

Seb. What hope can there remain ? I follow'd her
flight fo clofe, that in a few Hours we came up with the
Veffel, in which, I was affur'd, fhe went; but before we
had hail'd 'em, a Storm arofe, that feparated us; I faw
that Veffel fink, and the Plank on which you found me,
was all that was left of ours.

Rod. And why might not fome kind Plank remain for
her ? Sufpend your Sorrow for a while; and fince fhe was
bound for *Venice*.....
Tho' I'm proclaim'd a Traytor to the State,
Yet I have Friends here that I can command ;
They fhall imploy all *Venice* in the Search,
And ferve our prefent Wants, *Sebaftian.*

Pedro, (*Afide*) I'm glad to hear there may be Eating
towards.---

Seb. Rodoregue ! You opprefs me with your Generofity.
You left your ftated Courfe to fuccour me ;
And tho' your Ship by my ill Stars was loft,
Yet here you follow to another Shipwrack,
More dreadful than the laft.

Rod. Think not of that, my Friend,
I fear no harm, while I can ferve *Sebaftian* ;
Thefe Weeds, and your good Genius, will protect me.

Ped. Sir, Sir, there's a Lady that takes particular no-
tice of you. [*Enter* Villaretta, *and paffes over the Stage*]

Rod. I know her, fhe's a Widow, the greateft Fortune
n *Venice.*

Ped.

Ped. (Aside) Good! This may be a lucky Adventure--
Seb. She miſtakes me for another.

Ped. Ah! Sir, that's Grief makes you think ſo-- But a Woman never looks kindly upon a Man by miſtake, Sir, if ſhe had lookt upon me ſo, it ſhou'd ha' been no miſtake.

Seb. Cou'd not all that ſalt Water cure your Impertinence, Raſcal!

Rod. Let him alone, honeſt *Pedro*--- If you'll take a turn in theſe Walks, I'll try the temper of my Friends---- In the mean time, leſt you ſhould have occaſion for Money, take this Purſe, and uſe it as your own; 'tis all I ſav'd from the mercileſs Storm.

Seb. This *Rodoregue*---

Rod. No Words, *Sebaſtian*, with a Man ſo proud to ſerve you; Fortune has made amends for her ill Nature, ſince by it ſhe has given me an opportunity of knowing you. *(Exit* Rodoregue *)*

Seb. This Generous Fellow confounds me more than my ill Fortune--- *(looking on the Purſe)*

Ped. Talk not of ill Fortune, Sir, with ſuch a Mark of her Favour-- I cou'd no more grieve, than be ſober, with all that about me-- I wiſh he had told you too, Sir, where that rich Widow lives, for I long to be ſerving your Honour by Land.

Seb. Pray, Sir, let me have no more of your Familiarities-- Wait here till I return, Hang-Dog! *(Exit* Seb.*)*

Ped. Very pretty--! When we were ſinking, it was, Good *Pedro!* Dear *Pedro!* Segnior *Pedro!* Is there any Hopes--? He knew Death made all People alike, and thought fit to be acquainted with me, when he found we were near it-- If I cou'd but hang my ſelf now, I ſhou'd be as great as *Alexander*-- But I don't love Preferment at that rate neither-- What is there in this *Sebaſtian* more than in me? He can afford to be Idle, Game, and Wench more than I-- But I love it as well-- I was certainly got by a great Man, for I han't one of your Tradeſmanly Virtues, of Cheating, Lying, and good Husbandry-- So I'll
e'en

e'en get rid of this whimsical Master of mine, and push my Fortune. *(Exit Strutting)*

Enter Cæsario, *follow'd by* Villaretta's *Footman at a distance.*

Foot. Here he is---! Now what Trick will he have to get off---? Sir, Sir.

Cæs. What's your business, Friend?

Foot. My business, Sir, is with your Worship's little Finger.

Cæs. What does the Fellow mean?

Foot. *(Aside)* Ha! ha! right! He knows nothing of the matter-- Why, Sir, I have brought an old Acquaintance of it here, that's all, that you left with my Lady *Vil.*

Cæs. A Ring--! *(Aside)* What can this mean--! I left no Ring, Friend, and none will I receive.

Foot. Ha! ha! ha! Right again-- *(Aside)* My Lady said, Sir, that you wou'd have the Modesty to disown it, ha! ha--! But to advise you as a Friend, Sir, you must lay your Baits better, or you'ill catch no Fish in our Ponds-- There, Sir, take it; so you threw it, and so it is return'd-- *(going, and returns)* I forgot one thing, Sir, she says, if you can excuse your doings, you may call to morrow, but your Ring-plots won't take, Sir, ha! ha! ha! *(Aside)* Left no Ring-- A Rogue! *(Exit)*

Cæs. *(takes up the Ring)* Ha! A rich Brillon! What's her Design--? Now I reflect, she view'd me with uncommon Curiosity: Pray Heaven, my Out-side has not charm'd her--! It must be so-- How easily a Woman is deceiv'd, when the Deluder's Man--! Poor Lady! You had better take the Lord you hate into your Arms, than me-- You'll lose your Lover when you find him, and like the rest of the World, when you have got your Happiness, be farthest from it.

> *On this alone depends most Human Bliß,*
> *When kindly Heaven forbids us what we Wish.*

End of the second A C T.

A C T.

A C T III.

Enter Emilia, Dromia, *and* Drances.

Dra. HEre! Here! Fix your felves behind the Arras, and fummon all the Malice of your Sex to keep you from laughing.

Em. O! Fear us not, we're too well pleas'd with your Plot, to interrupt it.

Dro. I'm charm'd with it! Why you'll reconcile us to your Liquor, if thefe are the effects on't.

Dra. That wou'd be too condefcending, Madam, for Claret is infinitely fmaller than Tea.

Em. Nay, now you're rude Coufen.

Dro. I can forgive Segnior *Drances* greater Crimes.

Dra. Oh! Madam---! But your Ladyfhip is fo charming, and withal fo good; that I take an infinite delight to exercife your Mercy.

Dro. And they that cou'd withold it from you, muft not have a Breaft like mine.

Em. (*Afide*) A loving old Woman, is worfe than a hopeful old Man. Ha! ha! to languifh at Sixteen. I'd as foon pray at Sixteen.......

Dro. But is it poffible you cou'd perfwade him to think fhe has a Paffion for his Perfon?

Dra. Retire but a moment, Madam, and you'll fee, for I hear him coming.

Em. If he fhou'd come to lofe his Place for his Love, this Bufinefs wou'd end too cruelly.

Dra. I have a Salvo for that, Coz. It fhall be nothing but Mirth--- So along.

Dro. Nothing but Mirth, I'll engage. *(they go behind the Scenes)* [*Enter* Taquilet.]

Dra. Taquilet!

E   *Taq.*

Taq. Dear Segnior *Drances!* I'm so overjoy'd at the greatness of my good Fortune, that I have quite forgot the unlikelyhood of its being true.

Dra. There is none, *Taquilet*--- Women have had their Freaks in all Ages, *Læda* fell in Love with a Swan; *Europa* with a Bull; and can a Lady be disgrac'd with a Butler?

Taq. Not in the least Segnior! And I'll give her the best of my Cellar, I warrant--- Nay, I have Noble Blood in my Veins too, for my Father had a Velvet-Pall at his Funeral.

Dra. She knows it, Man-- Besides, did not my Lady *Brawn* marry her Coach-man, and the divorc'd Lady *Spare-none,* an Attorney's-Clerk?

Taq. Ha! ha! Right! Little Segnior, my merry Cousen, that must be -- I'm resolv'd when I am marry'd, to do something for you.

Dra. Dear--- *(Aside)* Rascal.

Taq. But I'm afraid you have too much Wit to make a great Man-- Yet I'll prefer you, and make you my Secretary the first Dash, for I can't write my self.

Dra. Oh! A Man of your Quality will be above it.

Taq. That must be true, for the very Expectation of Greatness, has spoil'd me for Business, and now if I an't a Gentleman, I shall be fit for nothing-- But, dear Segnior! Cousen, I mean, how must I behave my self before the Priest?

Dra. Puh! That will happen as it does at other Weddings; you'll look as if you were taking Orders, and she'll look as if she was taking Physick.

Taq. So all our Lives after will be Preaching and Spewing?

Dra. Ha! ha! Why you have been marry'd already, *Taquilet?*

Taq. Never, by the Mass! But I love to know.

Dra. There is but one Rule after-- And that is, when your Wife has the Spleen, she has been disappointed abroad; but when she strokes your Cheeks, and is very loving, you're a Monster, dear *Taquilet!*

Taq,

Taq. Why then a Man may tell to half an Hour when he's a Cuckold, by the increafe of his Wives good Nature to him ?

Dra. Right, *Taquilet!* And 'tis a Difcovery you fhou'd pray for-- For your honeft Woman is Proud! Infolent! Sickly! and full of Noife, to balance that one good Quality of being Chaft! But your other is Civil, good Natur'd, Quiet, and without Doctors, to make amends for one ill Quality that you never fee. (*a Knocking without*)

Taq. Ha! Who's that?

Dra. If it fhou'd be fome Rival? [*Enter* Cæfario]

Taq. A Rogue in Red! There muft be mifchief--- A handfome Dog too!

Cæf. I muft fpeak with the Lady of the Houfe.

Dra. What's your bufinefs, Friend?

Cæf. Sir, my bufinefs no body muft know but her felf, and her I muft fpeak with.

Dra. Sure you're fome *Italian* Prince in Difguife, or *Englifh* Efquire, you ftrut fo?

Taq. (*Afide*) I muft fend this Fellow a going--- Sir, you can't do your bufinefs then, for my Lady is bufy! Has taken Phyfick! And is faft afleep! And I'll tell you prefently whether fhe is not gone out. (*Exit, and returns*)

Cæf. (*Afide*) A very whimfical Family--- !

Taq. Sir, my Lady fays, fhe can't be fpoke with, and is not at home.

Cæf. Ha! ha! Then, Sir, I'll juft tell her Ladyfhip, that I'm forry I cou'd not meet with her, and go.

Dra. Hold, Sir, not without our leave.

Taq. (*getting behind* Drances) No, Sir, not without our leave, as Segnior *Drances* fays.

Cæf. Here fhe comes! Now Gentlemen without your leave. [*Enter* Villaretta]

Vill. How's this! Who taught you this Infolence! (*to* Taq.) --- Sir, I'll ask Pardon for my Kinfman's Folly, in the other Room. (*Exeunt* Vil. *and* Cæf.)

Taq.

Taq. Segnior-- *!* If my Lady was so in love with me, as you say, she's strangely alter'd *!*

Dra. Puh *!* All Women change, and at all times ; so 'tis but to knock that young Fellow o'th' Head, and she'll come about agen, Man.

Taq. If it be so, Segnior, I have a Toledo in my Trunk shall do his business ; for I'm a *Spaniard* by Nature, and can't live without a Sword and a Snuff-box.

Dra. Then you may use both, that is, blind him first, and fight him after.

Taq. Right, Segnior, there's nothing like Stratagem in War-- So march on to the Enemy.　　(*Exeunt*)

[*Re-enter* Cæsario, *and* Villaretta, (*a Couch*)]

Cæs. Madam, my only business now is, to restore this Ring, an idle Servant threw it me ; and thus I give it back.　　　　　　　　　　(*offers it scornfully*)

Vill. (*takes it hastily*) He that refuses it, deserves it not *!*

Cæs. Nay, Lady, all merit I wou'd want before you : I came to plead my Master's, not my own.

Vill. (*Aside*) Scorn'd by a Boy *!*
I wou'd resume my self, and stifle this fond Flame ;
But Love forbids.
The little Tyrant baffles all our Reason ;
And none can feel the Smart, and hide the Wound *!*
With a mysterious Cruelty he reigns,
That covers still the Innocent with shame ;
The injur'd wear the Tokens of the Guilty,
And falsely here, the Murder'd blushes,
Not the Murderer--- *!*
Yet who can look on him, and blame me ?

Cæs. Lady, I find this Ring amuses you, wore it any Charm that my returning has destroy'd ?

Vill. Perhaps it did-- And a Charm *!*
Against which the Base alone cou'd be secure.

Cæs.

Cæs. Then I thank my Bafenefs *!* I am not the firft that have been made happy by Vices--- But, dear myfterious Lady, tell me what you mean ?

Vill. Look on my Face, and you may read my Breaft.

Cæs. (*kneeling*) Ah! Madam, if I have any intereft there--

Vill. Ha *!* You have *!* Speak on--- *!*

Cæs. I bring a Heart big with tendernefs for you, that lives upon your Looks, and knows no Joy but in beholding you *!*

Vill. (*takes her by the Hand, and kneels too*) O *!* charm me on, Fair Youth--*!* Thy Words than *Hybla* drops more fweet. Infufe new Life into my Soul-- Where *!* O*!* Where *!* has all this cruel Kindnefs lain ?

Cæs. In Lord *Moreno*'s Bofom.

Vill. (*rifing quick*) Traytor *!* What fay'ft thou *?* (*Afide*) Under how foft Difguife will Villany lie hid ? I'm diftracted *!* I cou'd kill him *!* A Slave *!* A Monfter--*!* A Man--- *!* (*in a low Voice*)

Cæs. I beg for him-- What if obtain'd kills me......

Vill. Ha *!* What fay'ft thou, Youth *?* (*foothingly*)

Cæs. Too much, if you have heard any thing.

Vill. Fear not to fpeak, you fpeak before your Friend.

Cæs. I fhall betray the Caufe I come to plead---- I dare not fpeak.

Vill. Forgive me Sir, I mifinterpreted your Carriage-- Then it is only fear of his Succefs diftracts you ?

Cæs. Nothing elfe, I affure you.

Vill. (*takes her Hand*) I'm happy yet--*!*
That Jealoufy is kind as it is groundlefs.
O *!* Let me here unfold my Bofom to you,
Shew you the Secret of my Soul, my pleafing Cares---
And tendereft Wifhes--- *!*
Defpife not, gentle Youth, a Victory
That coft fo little-- to you of all Mankind,
An eafy Victory--*!*

Cæs,

Caf. (*Afide*) Poor Lady--*!*

Vill. Hide a Woman's Blufhes--- Turn not from me, nor upbraid me with your Eyes---

Caf. (*Afide*) I pity her, yet dare not help her.

Vill. Here *!* Look on this, it is my Picture-- That does not blufh, but may grow pale, if you fhou'd ufe it as you did the Ring.

Caf. I will not, Madam, for I'll not receive it, nor muft I hear you more.   (*Exit running*)

Vill. Ha *!* Inhuman *!* You furely fuck'd a Tygrefs, And with the Milk, its cruel Nature drew *!*
---- I cannot curfe him--- Fare thee well *!*
Such Charms, the coldeft Bofom wou'd betray:
" A Fiend like thee, might bear my Soul away *!*
            (*lies down on the Couch*)

Em. Ha *!* ha *!* ha *!* *Villaretta!*   (*Enter* Emilia)

Vill. Who's that ?

Em. The happieft Woman in the World, is fhe that is a little handfome, no Fool, and that never loves, ha *!* ha *!* ha *!*

Vill. Don't triumph, good *Emilia.*

Em. You'll own then, that a Woman's Refolution to avoid Men, lafts no longer than fhe can meet with one that fhe likes.

Vill. Any thing *!* I'll own her Piety, her Vertue, lafts no longer, if you'll fpare me now.

Em. You need not fear Quarter from a Heart of Seventeen.
    Like you, the Pains of mighty Love I've known,
    And learn to pity Woes fo like my own.

Vill. Generous *Emilia!* You fee Love laughs at all our good Purpofes, and will be obey'd in fpite of Pennances and Cloyfters.

Em. Ay *!* We can't Diet it away *!* 'Tis a Fever of the Mind, that all the Water-gruel in the World won't prevent.- But how deep is your Wound ?

Vill. Mortal *!* Except he that gave it me will fearch it.

Em. So much Beauty, and fo much Gold too, *Villaretta* may defpair of nothing amongft Men.

                                Vill.

ill. 'Twill make 'em do any thing but that indeed in all Countries ; you may bribe a *Dutch*-man to fight, a *Spaniard* to forge, and an *Enlifh*-man to betray his Country ; but for Love, *Emilia*, there is no Bribe, and the Affections are always honeſt.

Em. You may bribe 'em to flatter you, and that's better.

Vill. How ! Than to love in earneſt ! Sigh for you indeed ! And value none but you ?

Em. Infinitely ! For when a Fellow loves in earneſt, he does a thouſand ſottiſh things, out of his impertinent Care of you ; whereas, Flattery has all the good Breeding of Love, without the Folly, then you may part too without the Tears and Convulſions of your true Lovers.

Vill. Puh ! Every thing is in the power of a gay Humour-- But Satyr, *Emilia*, is the Vice of Wit, as Bullying is of Courage ; the Love it abuſes, wou'd teach it to be Gentle ! Good-natured ! Kind ! Sincere--! That only Cordial-drop that ſweetens Life, and gives us Joys which are ally'd to Heaven.

> *For all we know of what they do above,*
> *Is that they Sing, and that they Love.*

Em. Ha ! ha ! ha ! To be told that *Villaretta* talk'd thus ! I ſhou'd as ſoon ſuſpect a Prieſt wou'd Preach againſt Pluralities, a Phyſitian againſt Atheiſm, or a Woman hate Detraction--! You that uſe to laugh at all Lovers, to become one !

(*Sings*)

> Cloe *met Love for his* Pſiche *in Fears,*
> *She play'd with his Dart, and ſmil'd at his Tears,*
> *Till feeling at length the Poyſon it keeps ;*
> *Cupid he ſmiles ! and* Cloe *ſhe weeps !*

Vill. This is ſome amends for your ill Nature-- Well ! There is nothing ſo right, and ſince you know my Grief, you muſt aſſiſt me in the Remedy.

Em.

Em. The propereſt Perſon in the World to adviſe with for your true Phyſitian, ſhou'd always have felt the Diſeaſes he's to cure.

Vill. That wou'd make 'em fit for nothing, but to give Phyſick which might not be ſo proper.　　　*Exeunt.*

Enter Drances, *and* Taquilet.

Dra. I told you, Courage, as well as Truth, lay in the ſecond Bottle; and there's no other way to the Duello, *Taquilet*-- What loſe your Miſtreſs for a prick in the Guts!

Taq. Not I, Segnior, if you'll ſtand by me.

Dra. As faithfully as if thou wert a Hogſhead of Claret——— I'll never ſtir while there's a drop of Red within thee ——— Here he comes.　　　[*Enter* Cæſ.]

Cæſ. They talk of fighting, I'm afraid to go by 'em.

Taq. (Aſide) That damn'd Red-coat ſtartles me-- He looks ſo like Murder, that I can think of nothing but boil'd Hearts, and Throats cut from Ear to Ear.

Dra. What, a Qualm already?

Taq. Not in the leaſt, Segnior! I was only thinking if I ſhou'd kill this Raſcal, in the height of my Rage, 'twou'd grieve me to be hang'd for him--- This curſed Law is what I fear.

Dra. When you're marry'd, you'll be too rich for the Law, *Taquilet*--! Juſtice, and the foul Diſeaſe, hurts no body but the Poor--! Come, I'll give him the Lie by way of Challenge.

Taq. Hold, Segnior, don't be uncivil neither.

Dra. (going up to Cæſ. *)* Sir---

Cæſ. Have you any buſinſs with me, Sir,

Dra. I come to tell you, Sir, that if you value your Life, be upon your guard.

Cæſ. S-- S-- Sir!

Dra. Unkennel Bilboe out of hand-- For thy Adverſary gives no Quarter.

Cæſ.

Cæf. You miſtake, Sir, no body has a Quarrel to me, for I have wrong'd no Man.

Dra. If you had, Sir, he'd ha' went to Law with you-- But he fights becauſe he does not know whether he's wrong'd or not.

Cæf. Sir, I am no Fighter; and if this buſineſs goes on, muſt beg Protection of the Lady of the Houſe.

Dra. I'll ſee what he ſays.   *(goes to* Taq.) Come, *Taquilet,* cock thy ſelf at him, and advance. Tho' he's a damn'd Dog at ſingle Rapier, and can hit 'ye within a Hairs bredth of the left Pap a thouſand times together.

Taq. The Devil he can ! I feel his Sword already quite thro' my Midriff-- A Son of a Whore !

Dra. But I told him ſuch things of you, that have a-bated his Courage, and he deſires only that you'd favour him with one Parry, juſt to ſave his Honour.

Taq. Rot his Honour, and his Oath too : Z'bud, he'll mind it no more than one that takes it to ſave an Employment.

Dra. Never think it, a Soldier's Promiſe---

Taq. Is like his Religion, which is not to ſave himſelf, but to ruin others.

Dra. Why, he lives by his Honour.

Taq. As a Whore by her Love, that is, by pretending to love, for as ſoon as ſhe does it in earneſt, ſhe ſtarves.

Cæf. (*Aſide*) I have over-heard 'em, and that Fellow is certainly as great a Coward as my ſelf. I have half a mind to try.

Dra. Frown a little, I ſay, and look dreadful. (*to* Taq.)

Cæf. (*Aſide*) I can but ask Pardon at laſt.   *? draws*) Villain look to your Life---

Taq. (*runs over* Dra.) O Lord! The Devil! I'm kill'd--

Cæf. Ha! ha! ha! I thought they wou'd not fight, there was ſo much Preparation.

Dra. (*getting up*) This Raſcals fear will infect me, (*draws*)   Come then---

Cæf. S-- S-- Sir!   (*trembling*)

F   *Dra.*

Dra. Since my Friend is not in humour to divert you, Sir, I will--- Come on Sir.

Caf. (*kneels*) O good Sir don't kill me, I can't fight!

Taq. How's that? (*draws*) A Rafcal, to draw upon me, and not fight-- Death! and Canon-bullets! Let me come at him-- (*Afide*) If the Dog fhou'd not be in earneft, after all---

Caf. (*rifing*) Sir, I'll beg your Pardon for any thing I have done, but pray don't kill me.

Taq. Coward! What could'ft expect, after affronting a Man of my Courage, but to be run thro' the Body, and have thy Skin pull'd over thy Ears. [*Enter* Rodoregue]

Rod. My Friend oppreft! (*draws*)

Taq. (*Afide*) O Lord! I'm a dead Man yet. (*jumps back*)

Rod. If this young Gentleman has offended you, I'll do you Juftice for him.

Taq. (*Afide*) My Heart's funk into my Heel.

Dra. You, Sir? Why who are you?

Rod. One, whofe Friendfhip for him is more than Words, for I wou'd rifque my Life in any danger that might threaten his.

Caf. This Obligation, Sir, is more furprizing, as it is unmerited, and gives me greater Pain for my Safety, than I had for my Diftrefs - How fhall I repay fo infinite a Goodnefs.

Rod. You more than do.

Dra. Come on then, Sir, if you're fo brisk.

Caf. (*kneeling between*) O! Hold, for Heaven's fake hold. Rather on me, Sir, turn your Rage,
On me, the unhappy Caufe of this Misfortune,
Than bring fo generous a Life in hazzard. (*points to* Rod.)

Dra. Thou art as impertinent with thy fear as a Woman, and art the firft Male-Coward that did not love other Peoples Fighting.

Enter fome Officers of Juftice, and feize Rod.

1 *Offi.* Segnior, *Rodoregue*, we Arreft you in the Name of Duke *Moreno*, and the Senate, as a Traytor to the State of *Venice*.   Rod.

Rod. Ha——! Nay, then I am loft.

2 *Off.* Your Sword Sir ?

Rod. Take it Slave-- But be not you concern'd *(to Cæf.)* my Friend : I told you of this danger, and now there is no Remedy-- What grieves me moft in this Calamity, is, that it will hinder me from ferving you, and make me leffen what I have done-- I blufh to ask you for part of what I gave you ———

1 *Off.* Come, Sir, away.

Rod. Yet I muft intreat of you fome of that **Money,** it was all I had.

Cæf. What Money, Sir ?
" For the fair Kindnefs you have fhewn me here
As well as prompted by your prefent Trouble,
" I'll make divifion of my Coffer with you ;
" My having is not much-- Here's half I'm Mafter of.
(offers fome Silver)

Rod. Ha ! Is it poffible; can you then
For the vile Profit of a little Gold,
The Wages of a Slave ; Reward of Villains-- *(pointing firft*
to the Officers, then to Drances)
Diffolve the facred Ties of Honour ;
And to your Intereft facrifice your Friend
You put me on a painful Task,
To upbraid you with my Services.

Cæf. I know of none but what you now did for me ;
" Nor know I you by Voice, or any Feature :
" I hate Ingratitude more than Lying,
More than Vanity hates concealment,
Or Shame the Light.

Rod. O ! Heavens themfelves !

2 *Off.* Sir, we can't ftay.

Rod. But a moment.
This very Youth I refcued from a Shipwrack ;
" Reliev'd him with fuch Sanctity of Love,
That tho' I'm made a Traytor to the State ;

F 2

Yet

Yet to favour his Defigns, I ventur'd
To land him here in *Venice*.

Cæf. (*Afide*) He fpeaks as if he believ'd what he faid.

1 *Offi.* Sir, this is not our bufinefs, we'll ftay no longer, Sir.

Rod. I go-- For his fake-- I'll remove my Eyes,
In pity to the Pains the Guilty always feel
Before the Injur'd-- Farewel *Sebaftian*. (*Ex. Offi. and* Rod.)

Cæf. (*Afide*) Ha! He nam'd *Sebaftian*.
Thefe Accidents have then befall'n my Brother!
Shipwrack'd! Wretched! My Woes fall thick;
And I, perhaps, the unhappy Caufe of all.
I'm glad the Warrants at *Moreno's* Sute:
I muft not tell him the miftake; but yet
I'll plead his Caufe, and wipe away the Stain,
That lies upon my Brother's Honour.   (*Exit*)

Dra. Ha! I'm fo aftonifh'd at the Villany of this Boy,
that I did not mind his going.

Taq. Such a Coward too, Segnior; but I never knew
a Rogue, but was alfo a Coward.

Dra. To difown his Friend, and leave him in his ne-
ceffity, a Rafcal: I warrant he can't drink above a Pint
for his Share.

Taq. Let's after him, and beat him.

Dra. Come on, he deferves it.   (*Exeunt*)

Re-enter Cæfario *with* Laura.

Cæf. I'm glad I met thee, *Laura!* One can't have to do
with Breeches, I fee, without mifchief-- If I had not been
a Man of great Conduct, I had pay'd for ufurping that
bluftering Sex.

Lau. What has happen'd to you, Madam?

Cæf. Nothing but a Duel or two, which I avoided
with as much care as the *French* do ill News.

Lau. Some Lover of the Lady's, I fuppofe, has met with
you-- That wou'd be hard, Madam, to be kill'd for another's Miftrefs.

                                                    Cæf.

Cæf. Nay, it had been for my own Miftrefs, I affure you-- For tho' I pleaded for *Moreno,* yet I gain'd for my felf-- I figh'd for him, but fhe figh'd for me, *Laura.*

Lau, Mifchief on all hands! Ha! ha! I fhou'd ha' dy'd with laughing at the miftake! Sure, Madam, you were fo much a Man as to promife her fair?

Cæf. No, I had nothing of a Man about me at that time, for I wou'd not delude her.

Lau. You fhou'd ha' given her a little hope, to ha' been better affured of her Temper, for thefe *Venetian* Ladies are full of Plots-- Madam *Maintinon* her felf is not cunninger.

Cæf. Ha! Thou haft put a doubt in my Head, that I was not aware of-- If this fhou'd be a Defign?

Lau. I can put you in a way to know, Madam.

Cæf. Dear *Laura,* how? I'd do any thing to be certain of her difaffection to my Lord *Moreno,* my Happinefs depends on it.

Lau. She juft fent a Footman for the Duke's Phyfician, and I happen'd to anfwer him-- Now, Madam, tho' Ladies frequently fend for him, yet fhe never did before, and fince your Ladyfhip's fo good at Difguifes, I'll drefs you up, and you may pafs upon her for him, which is a fure way to get into her Secrets.

Cæf. I like it extremely—— But how fhall I do to talk like a Doctor, and give Phyfick?

Lau. No body does Ladies, you know, Madam, they only feel their Pulfe, and tell 'em a pretty Story.

Cæf. Then I have no more to do, but think of my prating Doctor, and I can't fail.

Lau. The beft Pattern in the World, Madam, for he had a Word and a Pill for every body.

Cæf. Let's about it quick; and tho' I have not feen the Duke fince I came from her, yet I'm fo fir'd with this Phyfical Enterprize, that I muft purfue it.

And if Moreno *does her Thoughts employ;*
I come like a true Doctor—— *to deftroy!*

End of the third A C T.

A C T

ACT IV.

Enter Villaretta, *and* Emilia.

Vill. I Need not counterfeit Sickness--- The inve-
nom'd Dart has spread around a Poyson that
glows within my Breast, and beats in every Vein.

Em. Come, come, sit down, and look sick--- If the
Doctor comes in, and finds you at shady Groves! and
purling Streams! He won't feel your Pulse, for there's
none of those Diseases in the Dispensatory.

Vill. (*sits down*) Well! Then what Distemper.wou'd
you advise me to?

Em. Any Woman's, there are a thousand! The Cho-
lick! Vapours! Whimsy! Spleen! Opinion----! You
can't want a Disease, no more than he a Remedy.

Vill. I'm afraid he has none for me--- *Cæsario* is not
one of his Medicines.

Em. Never doubt his Skill! A Physitian is as fit a Per-
son for this Business, as a Priest, or a Midwife. But then
you must use him like your Confessor, and tell him the
bottom of your Heart.

Vill. If he shou'd think himself dishonoured, and grow
too scrupulous?

Em. I'd as soon believe him too religious---! That is,
if you fee him well---- The unrewarded have a great
many Scruples.

Vill. He shan't want that, *Emilia*--- I'll give him a
Senator's Fee, if he succeeds!   [*Enter Footman*]

Foot. Madam, the Doctor is come.

Vill. Wait on him in--   (*Exit Foot.*)   Now for a
Colour of Sickness-- One must have some regard to his
Gravity, and not fall too quick upon the matter----

Em. By no means! He keeps his Coach, and you must
not talk to him, no more than fee him, like a walking
Physitian.

Vill. You are mistaken there, *Emilia*, for 'tis his Coach
keeps him--- They set up a Coach, as others lay it down,
out of necessity---   *Em.*

Em. He's coming, begin !

Vill. Hoe ! hoe--! But muſt it be the Vapours, or the Spleen ?   *(in a low Voice)*   *Em.* Soft ! He's here !

Vill. Hugh ! hoe--! Sick ! ſick !   [*Enter* Cæſ.]

Cæſ. (*bows very low to* Em.)

Vill. Doctor !

Cæſ. How does your Ladyſhip do ?

Vill. Very ill! Hoe !   (*holds out her Arm*)

Cæſ. (*feels her Pulſe*) Hum--! A little Feveriſh.

Vill. So troubled with Spleen all Day-- What muſt I take Doctor ?

Cæſ. Let me ſee--   (*playing his Cane againſt his Mouth*) Your Ladyſhip muſt do nothing, but drink me a good Glaſs of Wine, with a few Drops, that I ſhall ſend you, and you'll be as well as ever you was in your Life.

Em. (*Aſide*) I muſt get a little Advice for nothing-- Doctor, I'm troubled with a trembling at my Heart in a Morning, what is good for it.

Cæſ. O ! Madam, the only thing in the World, are my Drops ! and Blooding, and Vomiting, or ſo-- (*Aſide*) I don't know what to ſay next.

Em. Will you write me a Preſcription of theſe Drops, Dr. ?

Cæſ. (*Aſide*) What ſhall I do now--? Madam, I always make up my Medicines my ſelf-- Never truſt an Apothe-cary-- They're all Rogues, and their Shops hold nothing-- I never viſit a Lady of any Rank, but I leave her Cham-ber with more Druggs in it.

Em. (*Aſide*) I don't like a Fellow that won't let me be cheated as every body is cheated ! He knows ſingularity catches the Crowd, and thrives the better for not being a Rogue the common way.

Cæſ. I hope, Madam, we ſhall bring it to that in a ſhort time, that every Preſcription, ſhall be as long as a Bill of Lading of an *Eaſt-India*-Ship, and that none but People of Quality ſhall pretend to be ſick.

Vill. That wou'd be very obliging, Sir, to diſtinguiſh us ſo kindly ; for now every dirty Tradeſman, whoſe Wife has eat too mnch, muſt preſently ſend for a Doctor.

Cæſ.

Cæs. Who muſt take her by the Hand, Madam, tho' he brings away the Itch--! But Apothecaries have done this! I have made ſome advances, Madam, to put 'em quite down, out of an honeſt Indignation to their Rogueries, for I hate to ſee People of Quality abus'd....

Em. (*Aſide*) By any but your ſelf....

Cæs. Don't your Ladyſhip find a Languiſhingneſs in your Thoughts, and a Deſire to be alone.

Em. (*Aſide*) Hum ! He ſmokes her Diſtemper-- I'll withdraw.... Lady *Villaretta*, I have Letters to write, and muſt take my leave.   (*Exit*)

Vill. Your Servant.... Exactly ſo, dear Doctor.

Cæs. Then, Madam, 'tis certain, the Paſſions of the Mind have this effect on the Body.... Your Ladyſhip has ſomething that troubles you?

Vill. You have touch'd the very Spring of my Diſeaſe-- (*riſing*) And if you had a Medicine for that Doctor ! You ſhou'd out-ſhine the Widow-making-Tribe, And all their College Honours.

Cæs. Ill anſwer for my Succeſs, Madam, tho' it were upon the Duke himſelf.

Vill. Now, Doctor, you are truly a Phyſitian ! Your very Words have Balm above the richeſt Drug--! There is a Youth call'd *Cæs.* in your Family, do you know what he is?

Cæs. A Nobleman's Son of *France*... Further I cannot ſay—— But if 'tis he has touch'd your Breaſt——

Vill. 'Tis he, and only he ! On him employ your generous Art — And as an earneſt of my future Bounty —
                                      (*gives a Purſe of Gold*)

Cæs. Oh ! Madam——

Vill. No Words, Doctor--! Array'd with Beams like theſe, you are indeed *Apollo*'s Off-ſpring.....! The poor Phyſitian knows nothing.

Cæs. 'Tis doing violence to my ſelf, to take a Fee before I have done you good.

Vill. That, Doctor, belongs to a Bag of Ten thouſand more : Do you bring me Health, and you ſhall bear away the Elixir.   (*Exeunt*)

Scene

Scene *the* Ryalto.

Enter Sebaftian *and* Pedro.

Seb. NOT feen *Rodoregue* yet?

Ped. Nor any one elfe in thefe Walks——
The Duke has but a thin Table to day, Sir, no body
Dines with him, but your Honour and your humble
Servant.

Seb. Hold your grumbling Rafcal! you fhall Eat prefently.

Ped. Sir, you command me intirely——If I was a
Woman at this time, that would ftop my mouth——
All my fear was Sir, that if I had dy'd here, the Serch-
ers would a miftook my Difeafe, and laid a Courtiers
death to my charge; the Gout, or the merry Confump-
tion! No body'd a thought of a Souldiers death, Starving!
becaufe I have Money in my Pocket, and a Shirt
on.

Seb. Hum! a very ufeful amufement!

Ped. Alas! Sir, 'twas worfe than that for to divert my
Spleen——

Seb. Your Spleen Scoundrel!

Ped. My Hunger Sir, which is the fame Diftemper in
Younger Brothers——

G   *Enter*

Enter Villaretta's *Footman.*

Foot. Sir, Sir!

Ped. Ha!

Foot. You fee Sir, I'm come again!

Seb. Friend?

Foot. Tother meffage to you Sir.

Ped. [*Afide*] This fellow looks like a Pimp, there's fomething in the Wind!

Seb. Tother meffage! why I never faw thee before.

Foot. Ha! ha! ha! ha! good efaith!

Seb. Prethee Friend recall thy Senfes, for I may put an end to thy mirth, fooner than thou expects.

Ped. [*Afide*] My Mafter's fo dull of late, he fpoils every thing.

Foot. That is to fay Sir, I don't know you! nor am fent for you now by my Lady, to bid you come to her——

Ped. [*Afide*] Right!——

Foot. Nor your Name is not *Cæfario*——nor is this my 'Nofe! nothing that is fo! is fo!

Seb. No Sir, nothing that thou haft mention'd is fo, and thou art mad.

Ped. [*Afide*] I cou'd hang my Mafter now.

Foot. One of the Company may be touc'd Sir, but I wont name his Name, becaufe he's apt to be Angry——[*Afide*] Never faw me before!——

Ped. Harkie Friend, are you fure you was fent to this Gentleman?

Foot.

Foot. Why do you ask Sir.

Ped. Becaufe Sir, there is a Perfon in the Company, that wou'd not be fo backward to wait upon her Lady-fhip.

Seb. I'll break your head Rafcal.

Ped. Nay Sir, that is not fair, when you have no Stomack your felf, to hinder me from a good Meal.

Seb. Prithee Friend, now thou fee'ft thy miftake, leave us while thou art well.

Foot. If I left you fo, I fhou'd not be long well, for my Lady'd turn me out of doors —— Ha! ha! to come home and tell her I have been perfwaded out of my Eye-fight! Death! Sir, 'twas not two minutes ago that you was with her.

Seb. Art thou very fure of that Friend?

Foot. Ay Sir, and will fwear it too.

Ped. [*Afide*] This fellow can't be a Footman, he's fome Attorney's Clerk, by his Evidence.

Enter Drances *and* Taquilet.

Taq. Here he is!--there's for thee Coward! -- ⎰ *Strikes* ⎱ Sebaft.

Seb. And there's for you, and you *Villanis*! ⎰ *He and* Pe- ⎱ dro *knock*

Taq. [*Kneels*] Good Sir, fpare my life—— ⎰ *down* Dran- [*Trembling.* ⎱ ces *&* Taq.

Seb. This Slave is not worth Killing.

Taq. O! dear Sir, no! I have no merit at all Sir—— there are a Thoufand Ingenious Perfons that will come to the Gallows for their wit Sir, that deferve your Sword——you'll difhonour it upon me Sir.

G 2

Dran.

Dran. [*Draws*] Since a fit of Courage has feiz'd you, come on young Gentleman.

Foot. [*Kneels between 'em*] O pray Signior ftop! my Lady'll have you all Hang'd, if you hurt him.

Ped. Why art thou mad ftill?——don't fear Evidence, you may bring 'em off at laft, by Swearing they did not do it.

Foot. Here fhe comes.

Enter Villaretta *and* Emilia.

Vill. Hold, on your Lives I charge ye!

Ped. [*Afide*] Ha! what now?

Vill. [*To Dran.*] Muft it be ever thus ungracious wretch,
" Fit for the Mountains and the barbarous Caves,
" Where manners never reach'd——out of my fight!——
" Be not offended dear *Cafario*————

Ped. [*Afide*] Hum! She knows him too, as well as her Man.

Vill. But be thy Nature, gentle as thy Form,
That Parricide, with brutal violence had peirc'd
My heart within your bofome——
'Twas for my felf I Trembled.

Seb. Is this a Dream?
Am I or they miftaken? Madnefs fure
Was never fo Harmonious——all agree!

Vill. You feem'd furpriz'd, as well you may, at this uncurtious ufage————But gentle Sir, go with me to my Houfe, and there I'll tell you Stories of his folly, that I hope will make you Smile at this.

Ped. [*Afide*] Hum! She's for a clofe conference —— the bufinefs muft be done out of hand.

Vill.

Vill. Let me at laſt prevail with you.

Seb. Madam you command me. (more,

Vill. O Charming ſound ! that word tranſports me
Than all your Cruelties cou'd wrong before. [*Exeunt.*

Manent Pedro *and* Emilia.

Ped. [*Aſide*] A very whimſical Intreague. Now will
he never be able to perſwade her that he is not the Perſon——And I warrant ſhe'll examine every Mole
about him to be ſatisfy'd —— One can't gueſs how many Tokens ſhe'll know him by —— O! my dear!
theſe are the Lips, I'm ſure Kiſs't juſt ſo! and your Arms
met about me in the very ſame manner!——I can't
be miſtaken——pray put 'em round me once more——
exactly——Ha! ha! I'll follow, the whole Family
are of a piece, and 'tis very likely ſhe may have a
Maid that will ſwear me out of my ſelf too, and
examine my perſon with as much curioſity——Ha!
here ſhe is! ſtays for that purpoſe——[*Bows very low.*

Em. [*Aſide*] I have a great mind to ask the Man what
his Maſter thinks of *Villaretta.*

Ped. [*Bowing very low*] [*Aſide*] My Nimphs name I
ſuppoſe is *Abigal.*

Em. [*Aſide*] The Valet is commonly the Privy Coun-
cellour.

Ped. [*Bows ſtill*] [*Aſide*] *Priſcilla!* I believe by her ſi-
lence [*goes nearer and Bows*] Madam!

Em. [*Aſide*] O! he has a mind to ſpeak with me——
What wou'ſt have Friend?

Ped. Ah Madam—— ſomething that I dare not mention.

Em.

Em. What can that be ?

Ped. [*Afide*] Right ! —— { *Offers to take her by the hand,*
Why truly Child as you fay, { *and looks in her Face.*
what can that be?

Em. Ha! Villain ! what infolence is [*ftrikes him*]
this ? ——I'll fend fome to you that fhall teach you
manners. *Exit.*

Ped. Hum! my Miftrefs I find is not altogether fo
fond as my Mafter's——tho' fhe's more familiar——!
a Virago! a Man muft make Love in Armour, if he
has any value for his fore Teeth—— She'd make an
excellent Wife for a Dragoon——She'd keep him from
making Mufters, I'll ingage! [*Exit.*

Enter Moreno *and* Cæfario.

Mor. Thy words pierce thro' me, every accent flies
Loaded with mortal Poyfon to my heart ;
Sure *Venus*'s Son is deaf, as well as blind,
For every God, but Love, is mov'd by pray'r.

Caf. My Lord forgot her——She's a pevifh Beauty,
That likes her felf too much to fee your merit :.
Grief is for little People, may
Th' Illuftrious Duke of *Venice* feel no care.

Mor. Poor *Cæfario*! thou look'ft upon
The gaudy glittering out-fide of Power !
And feeft not the diffappointments, cares,
Anxieties, and impoffible wifhes that are under.
Curfe on the forward fool, that firft Ambition fir'd
To ftep above the quiet level of his Race,
Leaving happy to be great!——Had I not been a Prince,
Villaretta might a pitty'd me.

Caf.

Cæf. Say that her Heart's devoted to another,
As your's to her, or as fome Woman elfe
May figh my Lord for you :
Wou'd you then hope for pitty in her Breaft ;
Or wou'd you give it to the bleeding Dame ?

Mor. She is not to be weigh'd with common things ;
A Prize like her fhou'd be the World's difpute,
And Crown at laft Superiour merit.
What wou'd he do for her that I'd refufe ?

Cæf. If I were fhe, and judge of that difpute,
The ftriving World with fcorn I wou'd refufe ?
And throw the Prize into your Highneffes Arms.

Mor. Dear partial Boy !
Thou ftill haft fomething to delude my cares :
How fhall I reward thy kindnefs——I'll give
The any thing thou asks me.

Cæf. Thank ye my Lord!—Remember but that promife,
And I'm happy *!*

Mor. I'll give you inftance now *Cæfario,*
Of my good wifhes to you——You fay that
Rodoregue Refcu'd you, and is my Prifoner.

Cæf. He is my Lord, they call him *Rodoregue,*
And faid he was a Traitor to the State.
Forgive me Sir, for pleading for your Enemy ;
All that are yours are mine.

Mor. Lead to him *Cæfario,* and reft affur'd,
However Criminal he is to me,
His fervices to you fhall cancel all,
And leave me in his debt——

[*Exeunt.*

Enter

Enter Sebaſtian *and* Pedro.

Seb. "THis is the Air! that is the Glorious Sun!
" This Pearl ſhe gave me!--I do ſee! and feel it!
No ſhape of fancy, or deluſive dream :
A Woman too, that has Wit! that has Honour!
And Charms enough to make a Man upon
The Wrack forget his Pains! ———

Yet it is wondrous all! and Madneſs! ſomewhere
ſhe calls me *Cæſario*! cruel! and talks with the aſſur'd
Air of long Acquaintance! what can be the mean-
ing?

Ped. The plaineſt in the World Sir. .

Seb. Ha! have they told thee, unriddle *Pedro*?

Ped. Its no Riddle at all, I know a little of Woman's
temper Sir, for I was Pimp to my Lord *Midnight* before I came to your Honour, and when a Woman had
a mind to his Perſon or Money, ſhe'd rail at him,
trip before him, or write an angry Letter to him
for abuſing her———Now this Lady Sir, pretends to be
your old Acquaintance, that's all.

Seb. It might be ſo, if ſhe deſign'd a Gallantry, but
this is for Marriage, Blockhead.

Ped. Ha! ha! a Plot to put Love out of Counte-
nance; ſhe has ſo quick a ſenſe of this matter Sir,
that ſhe wou'd try to allay it with the Air of a
Licenſe, a Prieſt, and a Sack-Poſſet! Ay Sir, I wiſh
ſhe were in earneſt, for ſhe's the Richeſt Lady in
Venice. The Duke himſelf makes Love to her.

Seb. How can'ſt tell?

Ped. You know Sir, I am the humble follower of your fteps——and fearing I fhould betray you if I look'd like a Stranger, where you was fo well acquainted, I offer'd to fqueefe her Woman by the hand; but inftead of finding the great civility of her Lady, it prefently walk'd about my Ears at fuch a rate, that nothing but her Tongue cou'd go fafter.

Seb. She ferv'd you well.

Ped. She is the firft Lady's Woman of your Honour's Accquaintance, that did not admire a Man of my Breeding.

Seb. To the purpofe Rafcal!

Ped. She threaten'd very hard, but a compaffionate Footman took pitty of me, and carry'd me into a Sellar Sir, that holds the beft Cure of the Spleen in *Venice,* and over a Flask of it, told me the fecret of the Family——In fhort Sir, her Riches are as great as her Civility, and the Duke had rather Marry her than the Sea.

Seb. If this and fhe be true, nothing can add to my good fortune, but to find my Sifter Lives.

Ped. Saving that Sir, this will prove a lucky Shipwreck——Fortune's grown an *Englifh* Banker, and breaks you only to Enrich you.

Seb. Hold, here fhe comes——

Enter Villaretta *and* Prieft.

Vill. Blame not this haft *Cæfario*! if you mean well:
" Go with me now into the *Chauntry* by,
" And underneath that Confecrated Roof,
" Before this holy Man,

H

" Plight

" Plight me the full affurance of your Faith,
" That my moft jealoufe and too doubtful Soul
" May live at peace.

    Seb. None with your Eyes to doubt their wifhes needs;
I want no force where fo much Beauty pleads !
Let the good Man Lead on———
Before the Altar, I'll your peace infure,
And Plight a Faith, that ever fhall indure.

    Vill. The fumm of all my wifhes, dear *Cæfario* !
———Proceed good Father *!* Quick your bleffing give,
'Tis all from you and Heav'n I'd now receive !

                   [*Exeunt all but* Pedro.

    Ped. Hum! good Chaplain make haft———Ay ! fharp
fet, and don't care how foon Grace is faid ! If this Mar-
riage goes on, I fhall be a great Man! The firft thing
I do, fhall be to bring that infolent Jade that box'd
me upon her Knees, to fhow my power ; and I'll
Marry her after, to continue my Dominion, for I love
Gratitude extreamly———Then all the Imployments in the
Government, I reckon will be at my difpofal———I'll be
Secretary of State my felf, tho' I can't Write———But
to have a place, is to be fit for it, and to Receive the
Salary, is to difcharge it well———So look Important,
Signior *Pedro.*   [*Exit ftrutting.*

The End of the Fourth Act.

A C T

ACT V.

Enter several running over the Stage, crying out
stop Thief———After which,

Enter Rodoregue.

Rod. I Have given 'em the flip——But where can I fly?—— A lucky Fellow now wou'd escape, but he that's to be oppress'd by the malice of a Judge, has no chance———Ha ! ——— [*without———stop Thief*] 'llp etend to be Drunk, and so far at least shall look like an honest fellow——— Ti roll doll ———————

Enter Two Souldiers, and one of the Mob.

Mob. That's he ! That's he ! Knock him down, while I call the Captain——— [*Exit.*
Rod. Quarter Brother Souldier ! Quarter !
1. *Soul.* Brother Souldier Dog ! What to a Thief ?
Rod. Ay ! ay ! We both live upon Plunder, and are both Men of Honour———there's no difference.
2. *Soul.* How Rascal ! no difference 'twixt Souldiers and Robbers ?
Rod. None in the World Sir——Only we Rob for our selves, and you for another body, that's all.

H 2   2. *Soul.*

2. *Soul.* [*Strikes him*] Dog! muſt you be Jokeing with Gentlemen?

Rod. Sir. I'm your humble Servant.

1. *Soul.* Harkee *Tom*! let's inquire into his Pockets before the Captain comes, the Rogue wont feel——

Rod. No Sir, no more than hear.

2. *Soul.* [*Strikes him*] Why you Eves-dropping Raſcal, muſt you be liſtening to Gentlemen's diſcourſe.

1. *Soul.* What wont a Rogue do, that makes no difference between Robbing a Houſe, and Plundering like a Souldier?

Rod. I confeſs it is not to compare to Robbing a whole Country ———But I thought Gentlemen, it ſhow'd a Genious for it———A Man may come to Play at Cheſs in time, that begins at One and Thirty

1. *Soul.* You are merry Sir.

Rod. So ſays every dull Fellow, when he can't put the Mirth about himſelf —— But come Raſcals, I'll make you merry to——[*Takes a Box out of his Pocket*] I know your too much Courtiers to take Bribes, but every thing is yours that you fight for: So here's a Jewel in this Box——for him that can win it---

Throws it between 'em, which while they ſcramble for, he runs off, but is taken by the Capt. who enters at the ſame time.

Capt. Well met *Rodoregue*.

Rod. O! Barbarous Fortune.

Capt. She's kind to me, who had been loſt hæd you eſcap'd——The Duke is here———[*Aſide*] And muſt not know my negligence.

Enter

Enter Moreno, Cæfario, Rodoregue, *and*
Officers.

Offi. An't pleafe your Highnefs!
This is that *Rodoregue*! who with hoftile keels,
So long has plough'd our Adriatick Seas:
We found him quarrelling in the Streets of *Venice*,
Without concern or fhame.
    Cæf. Sir, let not that be in his Accufation *!*
My Danger brought him there ;
He Refcu'd me from the Infults of Two Ruffians ;
Drew on my fide, and fav'd my life.
    Mor. For that I am oblig'd to him.
    Cæf. But when he was apprehended,
He put a ftrange behaviour on ;
And fpoke to me as his old Acquaintance ;
With grave and orderly diftraction.
    Mor. Rodoregue ! what ftrang defign
Cou'd thus expofe you fingle to their mercy's *:*
" Whom thou in terms fo bloody and fo dear,
" Haft made thy Enemies ?
    Rod. Noble *Moreno !*
No publick caufe or enmity to you.
" A Witchcraft drew me hither ;
" That moft ungrateful Youth there by your fide.
" From you rude Seas, enrag'd and foamy mouth   (fake,
" Did I redeem, a Wretch paft hope ! ——For whofe fole
                           Known

Known as I was, a publick Foe to *Venice* :
I lay'd aside the cares of my own safety,
And here expos'd me to this adverse Town,
Where not an hour ago beset with Villains ;
I drew my ready Sword in his defence,
And sav'd a second time his Life :
But soon as the publick Officers had seiz'd me,
And I became the Wreck of Fortune's spite,
And in my turn his doubtless succour needed !
Instead of a stretch'd out Arm to save me,
Instead of drawing to relieve his Friend ;
He grew a stranger to my very Name !
And basely vow'd he saw me not before ;
Deny'd me my own Purse with pitty, for his fate
Had made me recommend this morning to his use.

    Cæs. With wonder and with shame I hear him speak,
I scorn to lesson what is done for me :
He sav'd me from Two Ruffians, and my breast
Is big with Gratitude for the Generous deed :
But I am still a stranger to the rest,
And still must vow I saw him not before.

    Rod. Exquisite Impudence ! This Boy wou'd make his
Fortune in a Court————'Tis pitty they shou'd loose so
promising a Villain !

    Mor. Hold *Rodoregue* ! you say you brought him hither:
When came he to this Town ?

    Rod. To day my Lord, and for a Month before,
(Kept back by Storms from making of the Land)
Both day and night did we keep Company.

    Mor. Distraction all, or vain design,
To raise the merit of your Friendship !

    Rod. No gallant spirit has so mean a drift :
I wou'd not Lye, as well *Moreno* knows,
I wou'd not run away——And 'tis

                                                 A

A meaner Cowardice to fhrink from Truth,
Than fly the face of Man.

Mor. Then thou art Mad, *Rodoregue* ! for this Youth
Has been thefe Six days in my Family,
The conftant Servant of my wifhes.

Rod. You too *Moreno* !

Enter Villaretta.

Mor. Hold this anon ! Here comes *Villaretta* !
Now Heav'n walks on Earth, and Beauty round
Invades us all ! Each glance devotes a Slave,
And every ftep, fhe treads upon a heart,
All of the Skies, but pitty you have brought. { *She draws near.*

Vill. Thefe Gallantries, my Lord, are loft on me;
So long you've play'd this old forbidden tune,
If I had ever lov'd it, 'twou'd a cloy'd me.

Mor. " Still fo cruel, Lady !

Vill. " Still fo conftant, Lord *!*

Mor. For ever fcorn'd !——Injoy the fullen pow'r
Of bleffing none——I will refume my heart,
Which all the Heav'n about you fhan't recall.

Vill. My Lord, I have no Heav'n or Stars to boaft off;
If I'm allay'd to any thing above,
'Tis in the Raptures of *Cæfario's* Love *!*

Mor. Cæfario ! ha ! Haft thou betray'd me ?
And am I made a Sacrifice to thee *!* [*Draws.* (wrong,

Cæf. [*Kneels*] Oh ! no my Lord, I have not done you
But I wou'd die to give you quiet.

Vill.

Vill. *Cæsario* fear him not! 'Tis I command you.
" Be what thou know'ſt thou art, and then
" Thou art as great as he thou ſhrink'ſt from. (ceiv'd me;
 Mor. [*Looking on him*] How has this ſmiling ſlave de-
And *Rodoregue's* wrongs are now too Evident:
But thou ſhalt pay for all.   ⎧ *Offers to Stab her,*
            ⎨ *Vill. ſteps between,*
 Laur. O hold my Lord, a moment ⎬ *and Laura Enters*
hold !   ⎩ *and holds his Arm.*

 Mor. Ha!
 Laur. Cæſ——ſa——rio——   [*Weeps.*
 Mor. What?
 Laur. Is a Woman!
 Mor. How?
 Laur. A poor unhappy Woman!
 Vill. A Woman Wench! Thou art diſtraɛted!
 Mor. What miſtery is this? A Woman?
 Laur. Yes my good Lord, I know it to be ſo.
 Vill. But I who know better, ſay he is a Man,
and my Husband————'Twou'd be ſtrange if I did
not know.
 Mor. Ha! Is this true?
 Cæſ. No my wrong'd Lord, I never yet was Wed,
Nor ever cou'd to her.
 Mor. This cloud grows darker.
 Vill. 'Tis but the baſeneſs of his fear before you:
Call in the Prieſt.
He ſoon will clear it to your Highneſs;
And ſhow the ſtrangeneſs of that Woman's Story.
 Laur. Madam, I'll die by what I ſay.
 Mor. I am confounded.

               Enter

Enter Prieſt.

Vill. Moſt wellcome holy Sir——
Father, I charge Thee by the reverence
Thou bearſt to Truth, here to unfold
What newly's paſt, between this Youth and me?
   Prieſt. A contract of Eternal Bond of Love,
" Confirm'd by mutual Joinder of your hands,
" Strengthen'd by Interchangment of the Rings,
" And all the Ceremony of this compact,
" Seal'd in my Function by my Teſtimony:
" Since which, my Watch has told me t'ward my Grave,
" I've Travell'd but two Hours.

Vill. looks pleas'd, Cæf. Aſto-niſh'd, Mor. Enrag'd.

   Mor. Now the Viſor's off abandon'd Hypocrite.
   Vill. Nay you ſhan't Kill him for his fear;
'Tis me he wrongs.
   Mor. He ſhan't another, Madam——

Offering to ſtrike, Laura holds him kneelling.

   Laur. Hold my Lord, don't Kill her,
let her be ſearch'd firſt, and you'll be ſatisfy'd.
   Cæf. O ſave me from his Rage——   [*To* Rodoregue.
   Rod. Begone Villain, and think not I'll protect thee more.

Enter Sebaſtian, *and Draws.*

   Seb. Rodoregue! My Friend in Danger?
   Cæf. [*Aſide*] My Brother!
   Rod. Sebaſtian, then are you?
   Seb. " Do'ſt thou fear that *Rodoregue*?

I

Rod.

Rod. " How have you made Divifion of your felf
" An Apple cleft in two is not more Twin !
Which is *Sebaftian ?*

Mor. Ha !

Vill. Which is *Cæfario ?* I don't know my Husband !

Seb. Madam, this holy Man will anfwer for
me.

Vill. That's more than you can tell, for he has already
anfwer'd for another.

Prieft. I verily don't know what to fay !

Mor. " One Face ! One Voice ! One Habit ! And Two
Perfons !

Enter Pedro *half Drunk.*

Ped. Terol dol ! dol !

Vill. Here's his Man, I'll afk him——Harkee Friend,
which is your Mafter ?

Ped. My Mafter Madam ! Why you're the only
Woman in *Venice,* by this time that don't know my
Mafter.

Vill. Worfe and worfe !——   [*Afide.*

Ped. He's very open hearted Madam, and if you'll tell
me where you Lodge, you fhan't live in Ignorance half
an hour.

Vill. [*Afide*] This is another Death to me.

Ped. But now I think on't, he has Marry'd a Widow
to day, and fhe'll take care of him the firft Night, my
dear.

Vill. Begone Rafcal !   [*Strikes him.*

                                    Ped.

Ped. Nay, if there's such danger in your fingers, I'll
keep my Master out of your Arms.   [*Exit* Ped.

Seb. [*Who has been viewing* Cæf.] Forgive me Sir, this
freedom, it concerns me :
But something while I look, diffolves my breaft,
And melts down all that's Man——   [*hides his Eyes.*

Cæf. What memory affects you Sir,

Seb. A Sifter's ! whofe very features yours ;
Tender and good as Angels !
Whom *Neptune* blindly in his rage devour'd :
For had he feen, he had himfelf been loft——
But curteous Sir, what Nation are you of ?
Did *France* receive the honour of your Birth ?
" What Kin are you to me?

Cæf. You call up all my fhame into my Cheeks ;
I've ftrove to hide that fecret from the World,
For what I do, difhonours what I am,
My Family is Noble, and my Country
The moft Civiliz'd ————
But leaft you fhou'd difcredit my account,
Behold this evidence of what I fay—— {*Shows the Mole on her Arm.*

Seb. [*Imbraces her*] My Sifter ! my *Viola* !

Cæf. Sebaftian!   (you?

Seb. Are you then living! how has Heaven preferv'd
I'm all aftonifhment and joy.

Cæf. Thefe weeds upbraid me now too much,
To let me fpeak————The Duke of *Venice*
Owns me for his Page.

Vill. And I thought too you were my Husband ?

Seb. Nature forbid the unfruitful Knot ;
She wou'd not, Madam, fill fuch Arms in vain,
And kindly brought me in my Sifter's Room.

Vill. [*To the Priest*] Why Doctor, we don't know
what we have done here!

Mor. " Be not amaz'd ! Right noble is his Blood :
I now recall *Sebastian*'s Family,
And if *Cæsario* be his Sister,
I must claim a part in this days fortune——
Cæsario, you have often said you lov'd me.   (of:

Cæs. I have my Lord, and now this Lady is dispos'd
I here confirm whatever I have said.   (mine;

Mor. You make me more your Slave, than you was
The merit of your Breast I lov'd before;
And if mine, Madam, does not appear
Less worthy for the Love it bore another——

Cæs. My Lord, it rather adds unto its value :
Your generous carriage to that cruel Beauty;
Your tender Passion ! and your constant Faith,
Increas'd at once my Love and my Dispair;
But since my Rival has another Blest,
That noble Honour, and that matchless Truth,
May now reward a heart that Loves you.

Mor. In that alone, I shall deserve it :
My Heav'n ! my *Viola* ! my *Cæsario* !
Let the dear Name survive ——tho' I discharge
The service—— And now you are
" Your Masters Mistress !

Cæs. My Lord, I'll exercise the power you give me
In one command ; that you wou'd succour *Rodoregue.*

Mor. If I had look'd that way, I had prevented you ;
Rodoregue shall share the blessings of this hour,
My present Service, and my future Friendship.

Vill. And now our Families are thus United,
Let's Celebrate our general Joy together :
A Mask was made to Adorn *Cæsario*'s Nuptials ;
It will agree, to which so e'er apply'd,

For

For I Marry'd *Cæsario*, my Lord, as well as you;
Sebastian is my second Husband——
   Mor. Then to *Cæsario* dedicate the Day;
Since 'twas *Cæsario* that has bleſt us all.
[Let the Mask begin.

After the Mask.

   Mor. Now the Adventures of the Day are over ;
We may look back with pleaſure on our Toils,
And thro' the various turns this truth obſerve ;
That Honeſty is ſtill the care of Providence !
   By *Rodoregue*, we ſee that good will wait upon a
worthy action —— By *Sebastian*, that Fortune can't
long ſtain an honeſt Friendſhip.

   And here I find, that ſome kind Star above,
Has ſtill a Bleſſing left for Honeſt Love.

The E N D.

Books Printed for, and Sold by *Geo. Strahan*, at the *Golden-Ball* against the *Royal-Exchange.*

SIR *Reger L' Strange*'s Seneca's Morals.
S ————Tulley's Offices.
A New Miscellany, being a Collection of Poems, by the best hands.
Letters French and English, by Mr. *Savage*, and Mr. *Tho. Brown.*
Memoirs of the present Court of France, and City of Paris.
Love Letters between a Nobleman and his Sister, in 3 Vol. by Mrs. *Behn.*
Mr *Dryden*'s Plays in Fol. or single in 4to.
Ladies Visiting-Day.
Love's Victim.
Modish Husband,
Inconstant, Or, the way to Win him.
The Patriot, Or, the Italian Conspiracy.
Love for Money, Or, the Boarding-School.
Rinaldo and Armida.
Boadicea, Queen of Britain.
Friendship Improv'd.
Fairy Queen.
With most other **Plays.**